SANTA MARIA PUBLIC LIBRARY

SANTA MARIA PUBLIC LIBRARY

3 2113 00751 1531

# Discarded by
# Santa Maria Library

j 629.13009 W947

Reed, Jennifer.
Wilbur and Orville Wright :
 trailblazers of the sky.
2008

D0573915

Orcutt Br.                    MAY 1 1 2009

# BRANCH COPY

GAYLORD

# Inventors Who Changed the World

# WILBUR AND ORVILLE WRIGHT

## TRAILBLAZERS OF THE SKY

JENNIFER REED

MyReportLinks.com Books
an imprint of

Enslow Publishers, Inc.
Box 398, 40 Industrial Road
Berkeley Heights, NJ 07922
USA

MyReportLinks.com Books, an imprint of Enslow Publishers, Inc. MyReportLinks®
is a registered trademark of Enslow Publishers, Inc.

Copyright © 2008 by Enslow Publishers, Inc.

All rights reserved.

No part of this book may be reproduced by any means
without the written permission of the publisher.

**Library of Congress Cataloging-in-Publication Data**

Reed, Jennifer, 1967–
  Wilbur and Orville Wright : trailblazers of the sky / Jennifer Reed.
    p. cm. — (Inventors who changed the world)
  Includes bibliographical references and index.
  ISBN-13: 978-1-59845-054-5 (hardcover : alk. paper)
  ISBN-10: 1-59845-054-9 (hardcover : alk. paper)
  1. Wright, Orville, 1871-1948—Juvenile literature. 2. Wright, Wilbur, 1867-1912—Juvenile litera-
ture. 3. Aeronautics—United States—Biography—Juvenile literature.  I. Title.
  TL540.W7R44 2007
  629.130092'273—dc22
  [B]
                                          2006033895

Printed in the United States of America

10 9 8 7 6 5 4 3 2 1

**To Our Readers:**
Through the purchase of this book, you and your library gain access to the Report Links that specifically
back up this book.
The Publisher will provide access to the Report Links that back up this book and will keep these Report
Links up to date on **www.myreportlinks.com** for five years from the book's first publication date.
We have done our best to make sure all Internet addresses in this book were active and appropriate when
we went to press. However, the author and the Publisher have no control over, and assume no liability
for, the material available on those Internet sites or on other Web sites they may link to.
The usage of the MyReportLinks.com Books Web site is subject to the terms and conditions stated on the
Usage Policy Statement on **www.myreportlinks.com.**
A password may be required to access the Report Links that back up this book. The password is found
on the bottom of page 4 of this book.
Any comments or suggestions can be sent by e-mail to comments@myreportlinks.com or to the address
on the back cover.

**Photo Credits:** American Institute of Aeronautics and Astronautics, Inc., p. 117; ASCE, p. 65; Carroll
Gray, pp. 19, 44; Discovery Communications Inc., p. 111; Federal Aviation Administration, p. 91;
GeorgeSpratt.org, p. 52; HowStuffWorks, Inc., p. 63; J. Y. Joyner Library, East Carolina University, p. 57;
Library of Congress, pp. 1 (portraits), 5, 10–11, 14, 21, 23, 25, 26, 30–31, 41, 42–43, 49, 50, 54–55,
56, 66–67, 70, 75, 87, 89, 92–93; 94, 96, 100, 102–103; Mississippi State University, p. 109;
MyReportLinks.com Books, p. 4; National Aviation Hall of Fame, Inc., p. 74; National Museum of Science
and Technology in Milan, Italy, p. 40; National Park Service, p. 106; PBS, p. 62; Shutterstock.com, pp. 1
(plane), 3, 6–7, 8–9, 16–17, 38–39, 60–61, 72–73, 84–85, 116; Smithsonian Institution, p. 35;
Smithsonian Institute National Air & Space Museum, pp. 12, 98; Steve Spicer, p. 79; The Aviation History
On-Line Museum, p. 77; The Franklin Institute Science Museum, p. 13; The Henry Ford, p. 18; The Ohio
Library and Information Network, p. 29; The Open History, p. 36; The University of Chicago Library,
p. 58; The Wright Experience, p. 81; Time, Inc., p. 97; U.S. Centennial of Flight Commission, p. 88;
Wright House, p. 46.

**Cover Images:** Library of Congress (portraits); Shutterstock.com (plane)

# CONTENTS

# MyReportLinks.com Books
## Great Books, Great Links, Great for Research!

**T**he Internet sites featured in this book can save you hours of research time. These Internet sites—we call them **"Report Links"**—are constantly changing, but we keep them up to date on our Web site.

When you see this "Approved Web Site" logo, you will know that we are directing you to a great Internet site that will help you with your research.

Give it a try! Type http://www.myreportlinks.com into your browser, click on the series title and enter the password, then click on the book title, and scroll down to the Report Links listed for this book.

The Report Links will bring you to great source documents, photographs, and illustrations. MyReportLinks.com Books save you time, feature Report Links that are kept up to date, and make report writing easier than ever! A complete listing of the Report Links can be found on pages 118–119 at the back of the book.

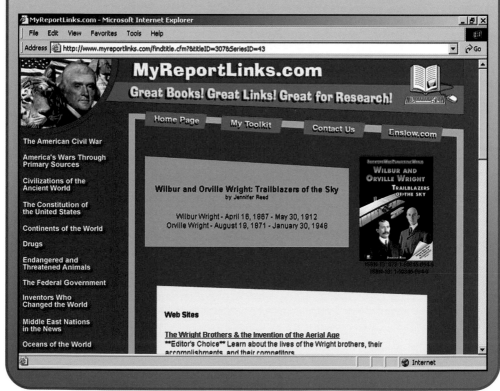

Please see "To Our Readers" on the copyright page for important information about this book, the MyReportLinks.com Web site, and the Report Links that back up this book.

## Please enter WRP1654 if asked for a password.

*"It is possible to fly without motors, but not without knowledge and skill."*

—Wilbur Wright

*"If birds can glide for long periods of time, then . . . why can't I ?"*

—Orville Wright

# IMPORTANT DATES

**1867** —Wilbur Wright is born on a small farm near Millville, Indiana, on April 16.

**1868** —Wright family moves to 7 Hawthorne Street, Dayton, Ohio.

**1871** —Orville Wright is born in Dayton, Ohio, on August 19.

**1874** —Katharine Wright is born on August 19.

**1886** —Wilbur is injured in a shinny accident.

**1889** —Susan Wright (mother) dies from tuberculosis on July 4.

**1890** —*The Evening Item,* a daily newspaper, is founded by Orville. Wilbur is the editor.

   —The Wright brothers open a printing business, Wright & Wright Job Printers, in Dayton, Ohio.

**1892** —The Wright brothers open a bicycle business in Dayton, Ohio, the Wright Cycle Exchange. The name is changed to the Wright Cycle Company a few years later.

**1896** —Otto Lilienthal dies from injuries suffered in a gliding accident on August 9.

**1899** —Wilbur writes the Smithsonian Institution on May 30 asking about additional publications on aeronautical subjects.

**1900** —Wilbur writes to Octave Chanute, author of the book *Progress in Flying Machines.*

   —*September 12–October 23:* The Wright brothers visit Kitty Hawk. During this time period, the brothers tested their 1900 glider.

**1901** —*July 1–August 22:* The Wrights return to the Outer Banks of North Carolina to test their 1901 glider at Kill Devil Hills, near Kitty Hawk.

   —*October to December:* The Wright brothers conduct further tests of their airfoils with wind tunnel and pressure, testing balances of their own design. They became the first investigators to compile tables of figures from which it was possible to design an airplane that would fly.

**1902** —The Wright brothers complete construction of their 1902 glider, which was designed on the basis of their wind tunnel experiments. They leave for the Outer Banks of North Carolina with their glider on August 25.

   —The Wrights make 700–1,000 successful glides with their 1902 glider at Kill Devil Hills. This takes place September 19 through October 24.

   —Orville and Wilbur start plans on December 15 for a new flying machine to be equipped with motor and propellers.

**1903** —The Wright brothers and Charles Taylor work on building an engine for the Flyer February 12–13.

   —Orville and Wilbur start to assemble their 1903 flying machine at Kill Devil Hills on October 9.

—Wilbur makes the first and unsuccessful attempt on December 14 to fly with the power machine from the slope of Kill Devil Hills.

—*December 17:* The Wrights make the world's first free, controlled, and sustained flights in a power-driven, heavier than air machine.

1904 —*April–May:* The Wright brothers build a new, heavier and stronger machine outside of Dayton, Ohio.

—*September 15:* Wilbur makes the first half-circle turn in air at Huffman Prairie Flying Field.

—*September 20:* Orville makes the first complete circle in the air at Huffman Prairie Flying Field.

1906 —U.S. Patent Office grants basic Wright patent, No. 821,393, for their 1903 flying machine on May 22.

1908 —The Wrights' bid to furnish a flying machine to the U.S. War Department for $25,000 is accepted on February 8.

—The Wrights carry a passenger on their plane for the first time, Charles W. Furnas of Dayton. The event took place at Kill Devil Hills on May 14.

—Wilbur Wright makes a public exhibition flight and first European flight at the Hunaudiéres Race Course at Le Mans, France, on August 8.

—The first airplane fatality occurs at Fort Myer, Va., on September 17. Orville Wright is seriously injured and Lt. Thomas E. Selfridge dies during the accident.

1909 —The Wright Company is incorporated on November 22, with Wilbur Wright as president and Orville Wright and Andrew Freedman serving as vice-presidents.

1910 —The Wright Company starts a flight school at the Huffman Prairie Flying Field in Dayton, Ohio, on May 5.

—Orville and Wilbur make their first and only flight together at Huffman Prairie Flying Field on May 25.

1912 —Wilbur dies at the age of forty-five from typhoid fever on May 30.

1913 —Orville begins tests on January 13 of the airplane automatic stabilizer, the last aviation innovation that he and Wilbur worked on together. The device was patented on October 14, 1913.

1915 —The Wright Company is sold on October 15.

1916 —*June–November:* Orville moves from the bicycle shop at 1127 W. Third Street into his newly designed aeronautical laboratory, located at 15 N. Broadway.

1918 —Orville makes his final flight as a pilot on May 13, flying an early 1911 model biplane.

1948 —Orville Wright dies at the age of seventy-six on January 30 due to a heart attack.

# Take to the Skies

The Wright brothers arrived in Kitty Hawk, North Carolina, on September 25, 1903. They set up camp on the sandy beaches. This area was a great location. It had soft sand, mild weather, and wind. They had been there before. Each year since 1901, the Wrights visited this area of North Carolina called the Outer Banks. First, they tested their kites. Then they tested their gliders. Now it was time to test their powered flying machine, the *Flyer*.

Many storms hit the area that fall. The Wright brothers had a hard time keeping their cabin or tent from blowing away. While they were forced indoors, they worked on the *Flyer*. Everything had to work perfectly if they hoped to fly.

It was a cold, windy day on December 14, 1903. Flying conditions were better than they had been. Not many people came to see the great event. Five lifeguards from the nearby lifesaving station became the ground crew. It was just too cold for other people. Many people did not think the *Flyer* would fly.

CHAPTER

1

Wilbur and Orville flipped a coin to see who would pilot the flying machine. Wilbur won. The lifeguards and the Wright brothers pushed and pulled the six hundred-pound flying machine to its position on a long monorail. The track was set up just below a high sand dune. Wilbur climbed on the plane and prepared for flight. He lay down on his stomach and tested the controls. Everything worked well. Now ready, the plane was started. It made a loud whirring noise and scared some of the people. The two propellers at the front turned quickly. The flying machine coasted down the track. Orville ran beside the airplane to steady the wings, but it sped up so quickly, he could not keep up. Then, Wilbur turned the rudder too sharply. The left wing hit a sandy hillside causing the plane to flip around and break into several pieces. Frustrated, the brothers picked up the pieces, headed back to camp, and started over.

It was only a minor setback. The brothers repaired the plane. They were ready to fly again two days later

This time the weather was not good for takeoff. They delayed the second attempt at flight until December 17.

The wind was strong, between 22 and 27 miles an hour. It was difficult moving the *Flyer* across the dunes. The track they laid down was 15-foot boards covered in metal. The Wright brothers jokingly called it The Grand Junction Railroad. The skids of the airplane rested on a board that was on a two-wheeled truck. It moved the airplane down the rail.

On this day, only seven people showed up to watch. Now, it was Orville's turn to be the pilot. Orville climbed on board and lay down flat on his stomach. He tested the controls and started the engine. The propellers whirred loudly, and the flying machine started to move. This time, it was on a

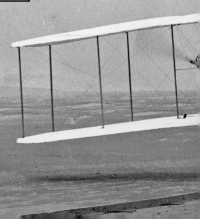

*Moments before this pioneering photo was taken, Wilbur was running alongside the flying machine, holding onto the right wing to balance it while Orville lay on the lower wing and managed the controls. Taken December 17, 1903, at Kitty Hawk, North Carolina, the image gave proof to the world that humans could fly.*

flat surface and was easier for Wilbur to keep the wings steady as Orville raced the plane down the track. As the plane became airborne, John T. Daniels took one of the most famous photos in history. Orville was flying! It was a short flight. He flew just 120 feet. It was the first powered flight in history. It was also the first controlled flight in an aircraft and one of the greatest moments in America's twentieth century.

Orville wrote about the first flight. "This flight lasted only 12 seconds, but it was nevertheless the first in the history of the world in which a machine carrying a man had raised itself by its own power into the air in full flight, had sailed forward without reduction of speed and had finally landed at a point as high as that from which it started."[1]

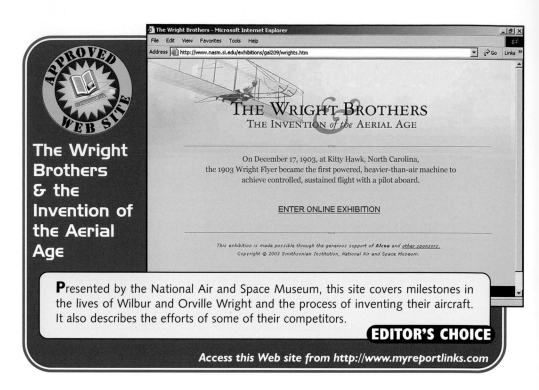

The Wright Brothers - Microsoft Internet Explorer

File   Edit   View   Favorites   Tools   Help

Address  http://www.nasm.si.edu/exhibitions/gal209/wrights.htm     Go   Links »

THE WRIGHT BROTHERS
THE INVENTION *of* *the* AERIAL AGE

On December 17, 1903, at Kitty Hawk, North Carolina,
the 1903 Wright Flyer became the first powered, heavier-than-air machine to
achieve controlled, sustained flight with a pilot aboard.

ENTER ONLINE EXHIBITION

This exhibition is made possible through the generous support of **Alcoa** and *other sponsors.*
Copyright © 2003 Smithsonian Institution, National Air and Space Museum.

The Wright Brothers & the Invention of the Aerial Age

**P**resented by the National Air and Space Museum, this site covers milestones in the lives of Wilbur and Orville Wright and the process of inventing their aircraft. It also describes the efforts of some of their competitors.

**EDITOR'S CHOICE**

Access this Web site from http://www.myreportlinks.com

Of course, the two brothers could not stop with just one flight. The cold winter air sent them inside their camp to warm up, but soon, they were at it again. They flew a second time. Wilbur would be the pilot. The second flight was similar to the first. Wilbur got the plane to go a little farther— 175 feet. The third flight proved to be the most dangerous. Orville wrote:

> This one was steadier than the first one an hour before. I was proceeding along pretty well when a sudden gust from the right lifted the machine up twelve to fifteen feet and turned it up sidewise in an alarming manner. It began a lively sidling off to the left. I warped the wings to try to recover the lateral balance and reach the ground as quickly as

possible. The lateral control was more effective than I had imagined and before I reached the ground, the right wing was lower than the left and struck first. The time of this flight was fifteen seconds and the distance over the ground a little over 200 feet.[2]

Despite this brief scare during the third takeoff, the Wright brothers conducted one final flight that would top the charts. Not only did Wilbur keep the *Flyer* in the air for fifty-seven seconds, he flew 852 feet! It was a remarkable distance for that time.

Tired and excited from their successful flights, the Wright brothers brought the *Flyer* back to camp. While they were talking about the flights, a strong gust of wind blew the airplane over. It

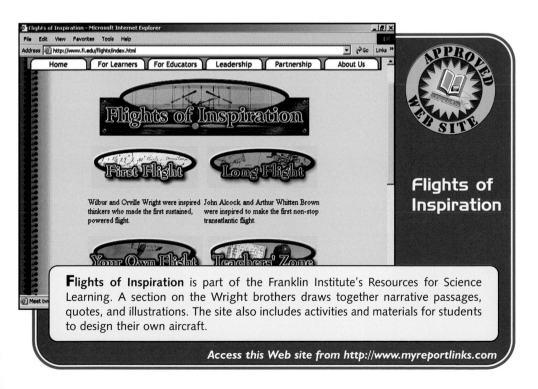

**Flights of Inspiration**

**F**lights of Inspiration is part of the Franklin Institute's Resources for Science Learning. A section on the Wright brothers draws together narrative passages, quotes, and illustrations. The site also includes activities and materials for students to design their own aircraft.

*Access this Web site from http://www.myreportlinks.com*

The Wright brothers were the first individuals to build an airplane powered by engine, controlled by a human, and able to sustain air travel. This photo taken in 1911 shows Orville soaring above while spectators watch from the beaches of Kitty Hawk, North Carolina.

flipped several times. John T. Daniels, who took the photographs of the first flight, tried to stop the plane, but it was too heavy. Holding on the entire time, Daniels tumbled along with the *Flyer*. He would later joke that he had survived the first plane crash. The wind that had originally helped the *Flyer* to fly now had destroyed it.

Orville and Wilbur Wright first told their father what had happened. They sent him a telegram that same day. It read, "Success four flights Thursday morning all against twenty one mile wind started from level with engine power alone average speed through air thirty one miles longest 57 seconds inform press."[3]

Orville and Wilbur Wright went home to Dayton, Ohio. It was time to develop their airplane. It had to be heavier and stronger. They also needed to make it useful.

On December 17, 1903, the Wright brothers proved to the world that humans could fly!

# CHILDHOOD DREAMS

The Wright family was a large and loving family. Bishop Milton and Susan Wright had seven children. Five survived to adulthood: Reuchlin, Lorin, Wilbur, Orville, and Katharine. Wilbur was born in 1867. Orville was born in 1871. Twins were born between Lorin and Wilbur, but they died in infancy. Beginning in 1870, The Wrights lived at 7 Hawthorne Street in Dayton, Ohio.

Childhood for the Wright children was happy. Milton and Susan Wright always encouraged their children to explore and learn. They also let them play often. Milton Wright was very active in the church. The family was raised with strong biblical values. Milton was gone much of the time on church business. He wrote many letters to his family. Later, Wilbur credited his success to his parents and living in Ohio. "If I were giving a young man advice as to how he might succeed in life, I would say to him, pick out a good father and mother, and begin life in Ohio."[1]

**CHAPTER**

**2**

## INTEREST IN FLYING MACHINES

Wilbur and Orville liked machines. Orville loved one such gift in particular. When he was five, he received a gyroscope top for a birthday present. It could spin and balance on top of a knife blade.

Wilbur and Orville's first introduction to a flying machine came in 1878. Their father brought home a small toy called the Penaud helicopter. It was a windup toy operated with a rubber band. Alphonse Penaud was a Frenchman who came up with the idea of using rubber bands for power. Orville retold the story:

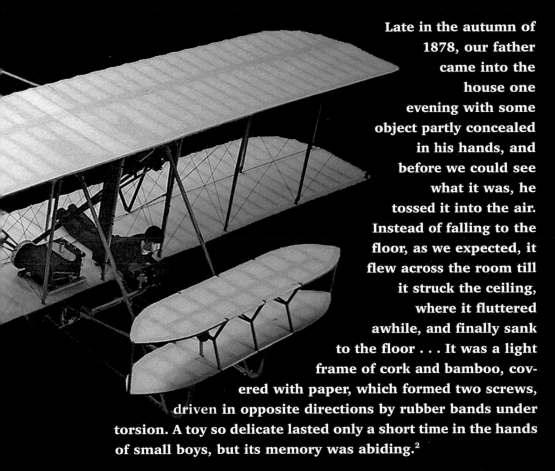

Late in the autumn of 1878, our father came into the house one evening with some object partly concealed in his hands, and before we could see what it was, he tossed it into the air. Instead of falling to the floor, as we expected, it flew across the room till it struck the ceiling, where it fluttered awhile, and finally sank to the floor . . . It was a light frame of cork and bamboo, covered with paper, which formed two screws, driven in opposite directions by rubber bands under torsion. A toy so delicate lasted only a short time in the hands of small boys, but its memory was abiding.[2]

The boys were so interested in this flying toy that Orville and Wilbur made copies of the toy. They called

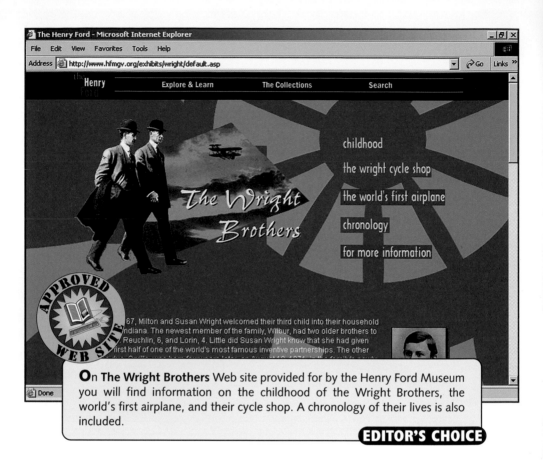

The Henry Ford - Microsoft Internet Explorer

File   Edit   View   Favorites   Tools   Help

Address http://www.hfmgv.org/exhibits/wright/default.asp

the Henry Ford        Explore & Learn        The Collections        Search

childhood

the wright cycle shop

the world's first airplane

chronology

for more information

*The Wright Brothers*

67, Milton and Susan Wright welcomed their third child into their household
ndiana. The newest member of the family, Wilbur, had two older brothers to
Reuchlin, 6, and Lorin, 4. Little did Susan Wright know that she had given
first half of one of the world's most famous inventive partnerships. The other

**O**n **The Wright Brothers** Web site provided for by the Henry Ford Museum you will find information on the childhood of the Wright Brothers, the world's first airplane, and their cycle shop. A chronology of their lives is also included.

**EDITOR'S CHOICE**

it the "bat." It always flew well, but when they made a larger version of the toy, it did not fly as well. The boys were just eleven years old. They did not understand at the time that the larger the flying craft became, the more power it would need to fly.

## ⇒ HUMBLE BEGINNINGS

By 1878, the family moved to Iowa. Both of the boys went to school, but Orville was a bit of a troublemaker. When Orville went to kindergarten, he went for just a few days. He decided to go to his friend's house, just a few houses down from his own. When Orville's parents found out, they were not too angry. The boys did not cause any trouble. They had busied themselves by playing with an old sewing machine.

Milton and Susan Wright encouraged their children to have hobbies. The children, though, had to pay for their hobbies themselves. The boys found odd jobs. Their mother would pay them a penny to wipe the dishes in the evening. Sometimes they did household repairs. One way the boys made money was by collecting and selling bones. They searched in alleys and old lots for bones. Then they sold them to

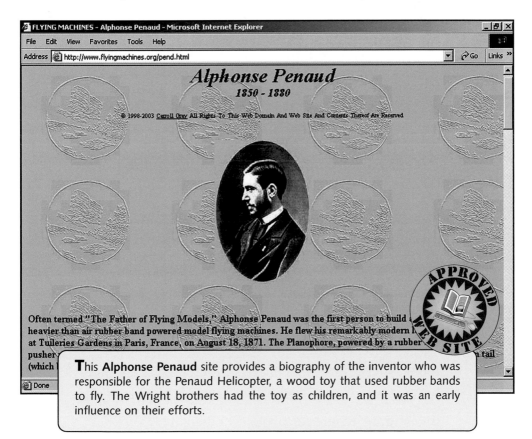

FLYING MACHINES - Alphonse Penaud - Microsoft Internet Explorer

File   Edit   View   Favorites   Tools   Help

Address  http://www.flyingmachines.org/pend.html

**Alphonse Penaud**
*1850 - 1880*

© 1998-2003 Carroll Gray All Rights To This Web Domain And Web Site And Contents Thereof Are Reserved

Often termed "The Father of Flying Models," Alphonse Penaud was the first person to build a heavier than air rubber band powered model flying machines. He flew his remarkably modern at Tuileries Gardens in Paris, France, on August 18, 1871. The Planophore, powered by a rubber pusher (which tail

This **Alphonse Penaud** site provides a biography of the inventor who was responsible for the Penaud Helicopter, a wood toy that used rubber bands to fly. The Wright brothers had the toy as children, and it was an early influence on their efforts.

a fertilizer factory, which made fertilizer from bone-meal, ground up bones. When that did not bring in enough money, Orville turned to kite making. He built and sold kites to his friends. He became well-known as an expert kite maker. He tried to make his kite frames as thin as possible. When Orville's kites flew, they bowed gently in the wind. He did not know that the curve of the kite actually helped it to fly. Later, this would be an important factor in designing and testing wings. Orville also took odd jobs folding papers for a church and selling junk. He even tried to make a sweeter chewing gum out of the bitter tar many of the young boys chewed.

## ⇒ HIGH SCHOOL YEARS

Orville and Wilbur attended high school, but neither received a diploma. Wilbur missed his commencement ceremony because the family moved from Indiana back to Dayton, Ohio. Orville studied special subjects rather than the curriculum for seniors. The library in the family's home and the encouragement they received to be creative helped the boys learn a lot. The Wright's home had two libraries, and reading was an important part of their childhood. Orville wrote, "Simply that we were lucky enough to grow up in a home environment where there was always much encouragement to children to pursue intellectual interests; to investigate whatever aroused curiosity."[3]

Wilbur Wright as a child. Although a very quick learner and passionate researcher, Wilbur never received his high school diploma.

Although the brothers were close, they had very different personalities. Wilbur was a serious student, and he enjoyed speaking in public. He was athletic and enjoyed gymnastics. But some would say he was a bit odd and not one to follow the crowd. He loved to read, especially books about flight and aerodynamics.

Orville liked to joke around with his family and friends. He once convinced a group of friends to throw gravel at their school's windows. Orville's class had been dismissed early, but the rest of the school was still in session. Orville considered himself the general of an army, much like Napoleon, whom he had read about in a book. His friends were captains and colonels. The school was under attack. They used clubs made from the school's picket fence. The boys were chased away by the janitor but never were reported to their teacher. Orville was very lucky. He could have gotten into a lot of trouble.

## ⇒ First Businesses

Orville quit high school. Because he loved to tinker with small machines, he eventually built his own printing press. Orville used old buggy parts, a discarded tombstone, and firewood. His press printed a thousand pieces of paper an hour. A printer stopped in to see the printing machine. He looked at it from the top, the bottom, and all different angles. He could not figure out how it

*Growing up, Orville Wright was known for his adventurous drive and mischievous nature. This photo dates to 1897, when he was in his mid-twenties.*

worked, but was surprised, because it was printing images on paper.

Despite their differences, Wilbur and Orville were close to each other throughout their lives. In the early 1890s, the two older sons, Reuchlin and Lorin, had married and moved out, which meant Wilbur was the oldest child in the house. At this time, Wilbur was out of school. When their mother, Susan, became ill with tuberculosis, she could barely walk. Wilbur took care of her and the house. He would carry her up and down the stairs and tend to the many duties of a Victorian house-wife. Orville and Katharine were still in school. This was a huge burden on Wilbur, but he loved his mother and cared for her for several years. She died July 4, 1889. Milton Wright said of his son, ". . . Her life was probably lengthened, at least two years, by his skill and assiduity."[4] Wilbur also had plans to attend Yale. He had taken additional courses in Greek and trigonometry to help prepare him for admission to this well-known university.

## WILBUR'S HEALTH SUFFERS

At the time Wilbur was caring for his mother and planning to attend Yale, he was also in a serious skating accident. Wilbur played a game called shinny that is similar to ice hockey. In 1886, when Wilbur was almost nineteen years old, a player on the other team let go of his stick. It flew through the air and hit Wilbur in the face, knocking out

Wilbur (left) and Orville (right) sit on the steps of their family home on Hawthorne Street in Dayton, Ohio. One of the great qualities that the brothers shared was their sense of humor.

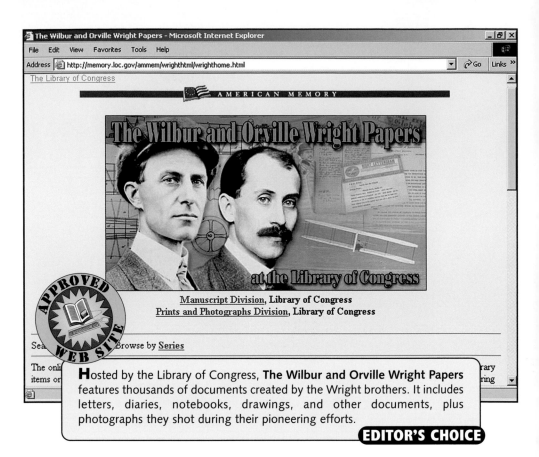

The Wilbur and Orville Wright Papers - Microsoft Internet Explorer

File   Edit   View   Favorites   Tools   Help

Address  http://memory.loc.gov/ammem/wrighthtml/wrighthome.html

The Library of Congress

AMERICAN MEMORY

The Wilbur and Orville Wright Papers

at the Library of Congress

Manuscript Division, Library of Congress
Prints and Photographs Division, Library of Congress

Browse by Series

**H**osted by the Library of Congress, **The Wilbur and Orville Wright Papers** features thousands of documents created by the Wright brothers. It includes letters, diaries, notebooks, drawings, and other documents, plus photographs they shot during their pioneering efforts.

EDITOR'S CHOICE

several teeth. A few weeks later, while recovering, Wilbur also was diagnosed with heart palpitations. His father wrote, "In his nineteenth year when playing a game on skates at an artificial lake at the Soldier's Home near Dayton, Ohio, a bat accidentally flew out of the hand of a young man . . . and struck Wilbur, knocking him down, but not injuring him much. A few weeks later, he began to be affected with nervous palpitations of the heart which precluded the realization of the former idea of his parents, of giving him a course in Yale College."[5]

Wilbur's poor health affected him badly. He stopped playing sports. Wilbur withdrew his plans to attend college and in the next few years seemed to suffer from other illnesses. Still, Wilbur did not idly waste time. He read as many books as he could and self-educated himself from home.

His brother had different plans. Orville was not nearly as interested in books as Wilbur, although he was just as smart. Orville Wright in particular loved to tinker with tools and machines. The Wrights' grandfather was a carriage maker. He showed the boys the tools he used to make carriages. Milton Wright also took the boys to see a large printing press. It was where the church published a news-paper, hymnals, books, and stationery. Orville was impressed by the machine and spent two summers as a printing apprentice.

## ⇒ PRINTING BUSINESS

Orville was well suited to the printing business. He started his own weekly newspaper and hired Wilbur as the editor. They worked with many local merchants. It was called the *West Side News.* Wanting to compete with the town's daily news-papers, the Wrights decided to publish one and called it the *Evening Item.* However, their daily newspaper did not last long. The competition from another more established paper was too much. The printing business lasted from 1890 to 1895. Yet, the Wright brothers were always thinking of the future. They were eager to start another more promising business.

## →Booming Bicycle Business

In the late 1800s, the bicycle was a relatively new idea. People loved to ride a bike because it was cleaner than a horse and much easier to take care of. The modern bicycle was developed in stages from about 1840 to the 1870s, and bicycles became the craze in the 1880s. Many people felt it was the greatest invention of the nineteenth century. The bicycle gave millions of Americans a new freedom—the ability to move about in a way they had not known before. By riding a bicycle, people could get places faster. It was convenient too. It did not require saddling or harnessing a horse. All the rider had to do was hop on and pedal.

In search of a new business venture, Wilbur and Orville started a bicycle shop in 1892. It was called the Wright Cycle Exchange. They sold and rented many different brands of bicycles. Eventually, the brothers designed and sold their own bicycles. Orville bought his first bicycle for $160. It was a Columbia safety bike, and he loved riding it. Orville entered races on his bicycle. Wilbur later bought a used Eagle safety bicycle for eighty dollars, but he did not race. The accident he had playing shinny and other health problems still bothered him. The name of the business was changed to the Wright Cycle Company in 1895.

The Wright brothers designed several bicycles of their own called the Wright Van Cleve in 1896 and the St. Clair. With these two new bicycles, the brothers also came up with two new inventions. In Dayton, Ohio, only a few streets were paved. Dust and dirt often built up on the bicycle's bearings and wore them out quickly. The Wrights created a way to keep this from happening so often. It was called the self-oiling hub.

Some earlier bikes also had a problem. As the rider pedaled, one pedal would tighten up while the other would become loose and eventually fall off. The Wright brothers designed pedals that would only tighten up and stay on.

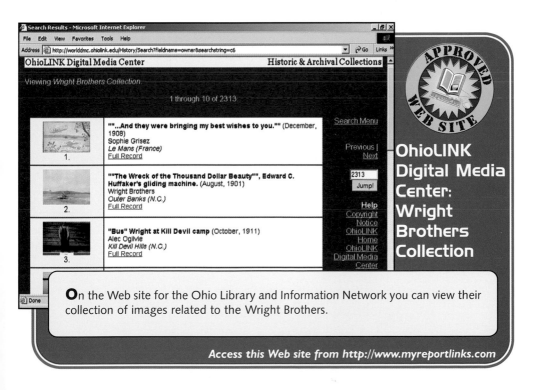

**OhioLINK Digital Media Center: Wright Brothers Collection**

On the Web site for the Ohio Library and Information Network you can view their collection of images related to the Wright Brothers.

*Access this Web site from http://www.myreportlinks.com*

This glider is flown by Wilbur (left) and Orville (right) as a kite. Three years earlier, Wilbur successfully tested a simple control system in a kite after realizing there were no suitable controls for pilots to use to balance aircraft in the air.

Business was great for the brothers. When the average worker brought home five hundred dollars a year, the Wrights each brought home fifteen hundred dollars. They were also able to save their money, which later helped finance their aviation experiments.

Unfortunately, the bicycle business did not last long. Bigger companies were able to sell bicycles at a much lower price. To keep up with the competition, the Wright brothers had to drop their prices until it was no longer profitable to stay in business. The automobile also changed the way Americans looked at transportation. With a car, people could sit comfortably and drive around. They were protected from rain, snow, and wind. Best of all, in a car, the driver did not have to pedal.

The Wrights sold their parts and the Van Cleve name to another bicycle shop. They turned their own shop into a machine shop.

## A Fascination With Flight and Kites

Orville had been making kites since he was a boy. Wilbur read books about flying machines, studied aviation, and became familiar with certain terms and inventors. Both brothers had a fascination for flight. Both wanted to build a machine that man could fly.

Wilbur liked to watch birds. He often rode his bike to a place in Dayton, Ohio, called the Pinnacle.

It was high up and overlooked the Miami River. Here, he could watch large birds like buzzards and hawks fly and move in the air. Later, while at Kitty Hawk, Wilbur kept a journal noting that birds could balance themselves in the air as they flew. "The buzzard, which uses the dihedral [intersecting] angle, finds greater difficulty to maintain equilibrium in strong winds than eagles and hawks which hold their wings level."[6]

Depending on the size of the bird, its shape, and the angle of its wings, when the center of gravity and the center of pressure meet, the bird is balanced and under control. However, it was not clear how birds did this. Still, like the great inventors before him, including Leonardo Da Vinci, studying birds was very important to understanding flight and something Wilbur loved to do.

## ⊜ THE WINGS

Past inventors could not keep their flying machines in the air. They did not know the secret of birds. Otto Lilienthal, a well-known inventor of the glider, thought that by swinging his legs back and forth, he would alter the center of gravity and keep his balance while sitting on his glider. It did not work.

It seemed to Wilbur that the problem was in the wings. How do birds maneuver their wings so they stay in flight? They bend or tip their wings to change their lift (ability to stay up in the air) and restore their stable flight. Wilbur realized that a flying machine had to be able to twist its wings. Previous inventors did not understand this. As Wilbur watched buzzards in particular, he noted that they could twist their wings. The bird would roll into the turn and stabilize itself. Wilbur also watched a pigeon. It wobbled side to side turning one wing tip up and the other down.

## →Back to the Bike Shop

Wilbur's understanding of how a bicycle worked also inspired him. Handle bars help to turn the bicycle. The rider also has to lean into the curve when turning. The turn is smoother when both actions are done.

Wilbur discussed this observation with Orville. They went back to the bike shop and found some things to use like an empty bicycle tube box. With his thumb and forefinger, Wilbur pinched the diagonal corners of the box. This caused it to twist or bend. He studied the twisted box carefully. The top and bottom of the box looked like the wings of a biplane.

To twist the wings means to bend them. This is called wing warping. The kite they designed had cables connected to the wings. These would be controlled by the pilot. In a plane, a pilot could turn or bend them up or down to turn the plane or gain lift. Today, airplanes do not use wing warping. They use ailerons. The aileron is located on

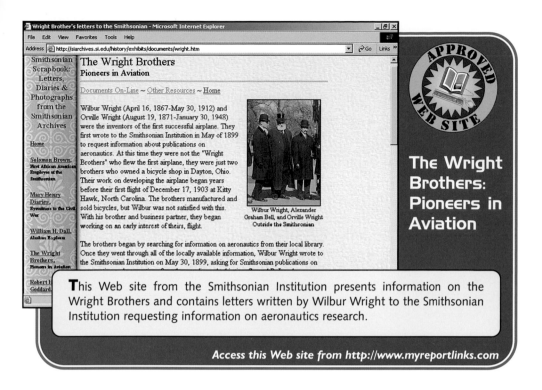

The Wright Brothers:
Pioneers in
Aviation

This Web site from the Smithsonian Institution presents information on the Wright Brothers and contains letters written by Wilbur Wright to the Smithsonian Institution requesting information on aeronautics research.

*Access this Web site from http://www.myreportlinks.com*

the tip of the wing and moves up or down. A pilot controls the aileron. If the pilot wants the airplane to make a right turn, he will drop the left aileron and raise the right one. This makes more lift on the left side of the plane. The left wing moves up while the right wing moves down. The plane makes a right turn.[7]

To test Wilbur's theory, the brothers created a kite unlike the ones that Orville typically made. It was a biplane box kite with wings that measured five to six feet long. It was made of lightweight wood and linen. The wings were controlled by cables. In July 1899, Wilbur tested the kite. It was a windy day. Two young boys, John and Walter

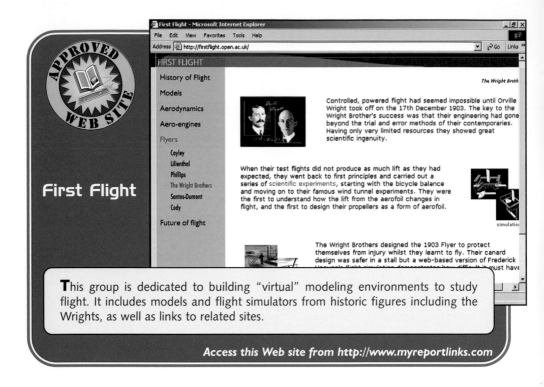

First Flight

This group is dedicated to building "virtual" modeling environments to study flight. It includes models and flight simulators from historic figures including the Wrights, as well as links to related sites.

Access this Web site from http://www.myreportlinks.com

Reiniger, helped him. Wilbur noted that when he pulled the cables to twist one wing up and the other wing down, the wing that was turned up had more lift. That wing would rise and the kite would turn.

Balancing the kite was also fixed. Tilting the kite one way or the other would change the center of lift. This affected the balance of the kite. The Wrights also added an elevator at the rear of the kite. The elevator was movable and controlled up-and-down motions. It is still used on planes today. The tests worked and the problem of wing warping and balancing was resolved, at least with the kite.

## ⇒ THE ELEVATOR

The elevator's location caused some problems. Originally, the Wrights put the elevator at the back of the kite. If the kite crashed, its front was not protected. Wilbur and Orville argued about where to place the elevator. Would it work best in the back or at the front? They decided to move it to the front of the kite.

The Wrights' elevator had three qualities not found in earlier gliders. First of all, it was in the front of the wings. Now that the elevator was in front, the plane was less likely to be damaged during takeoffs. Secondly, it created more stability and carried some of the weight, taking pressure off the wings. Finally, the elevator also controlled pitch. This means it controlled the airplane's nose moving up or down.

A final problem arose. Although the kite worked, it was not strong enough to hold an adult human being. Wilbur had studied Lilienthal's experiments with gliders. In fact, Otto Lilienthal, the father of gliding flights, influenced Wilbur and Orville. It was now time to take their kite to the next level. It was time to fly man!

# GLIDING INTO FLIGHT

**H**umans have always dreamed of flying. Watching birds take to the air and soar on the winds has captured our imaginations for eons. To be able to move so freely has been the fancy of many people since ancient times.

One of the first stories about man attempting to fly comes from Ancient Greece. It is a mythological story about a man named Daedalus and his son, Icarus. Daedalus was an architect, sculptor, and inventor. He was asked by King Minos to build a labyrinth for a man-eating beast called a Minotaur, which had the head and tail of a bull, but the body of a muscular man.

As the story goes, Theseus killed the Minotaur and was able to escape from the labyrinth. This enraged the king, who imprisoned Daedalus and his son Icarus in a tall tower. To escape, Daedalus made wings from feathers and wax. Using the wings, Icarus took off. He loved the feeling of flying so much that he flew too close to the sun. The wax melted, and he crashed in the water where he died.

**CHAPTER 3**

This story captured the imaginations of people from then on. The dream to fly led people to create some interesting flying machines. During the Renaissance, Leonardo Da Vinci, a scientist, inventor, and artist, was so intrigued by birds, bats, and flying that he spent many hours studying them. As a boy, he watched birds and bats fly around the countryside. He drew illustrations of wings and how the air flows over and under them to give the bird or bat "lift." He also studied aerodynamics, something virtually unknown during the fifteenth century.

He wrote in his books, "An object offers as much resistance to the air as the air does to the object. You may see that the beating of its wings against the air supports a heavy eagle in the highest and rarest atmosphere."[1]

Da Vinci's lifelong obsession with flying caused him to create some amazing flying machines for his time. His "ship of the air," as he called it, never took off, but in theory, it had potential. He also designed the first helicopter.

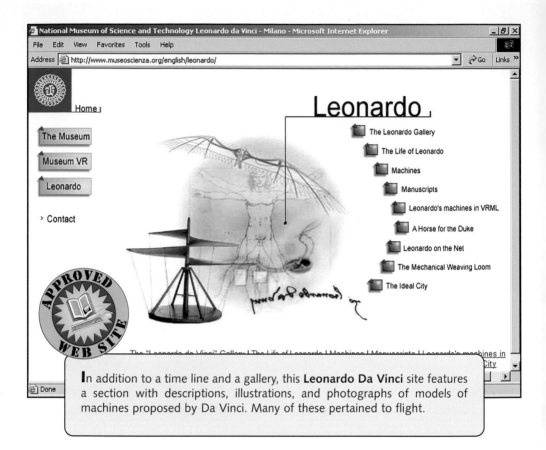

National Museum of Science and Technology Leonardo da Vinci - Milano - Microsoft Internet Explorer

File  Edit  View  Favorites  Tools  Help

Address http://www.museoscienza.org/english/leonardo/

Home

The Museum

Museum VR

Leonardo

> Contact

# Leonardo

The Leonardo Gallery

The Life of Leonardo

Machines

Manuscripts

Leonardo's machines in VRML

A Horse for the Duke

Leonardo on the Net

The Mechanical Weaving Loom

The Ideal City

In addition to a time line and a gallery, this **Leonardo Da Vinci** site features a section with descriptions, illustrations, and photographs of models of machines proposed by Da Vinci. Many of these pertained to flight.

The eighteenth century also brought its share of inventors. Jacques-Étienne Montgolfier, a French paper manufacturer, dreamed of flying in the clouds. He thought if he got a large enough sheet of paper and filled it with steam, he could create a balloon and float in the skies. In 1782, he tested this idea on a small scale. A small taffeta envelope filled with hot air floated to the ceiling. His second test on September 13, 1783, consisted of a much bigger balloon. It was 1,400 cubic meters and carried a basket. In the basket were a duck, a sheep, and a rooster. The flight lasted about 8 minutes, covered 2 miles (3.2 kilometers), and went to an altitude of about 1,500 feet (457.2 meters).

In 1783, a larger balloon was created, and this time two men, Jean-François Pilâtre de Rozier (a physicist) and François Laurent, Marquis d'Arlandes, were the first human pilots to fly the skies. They traveled about 5.5 miles (8.8 kilometers) for about 20 minutes.

Sir George Cayley is perhaps one of the most important figures in early aviation. His fascination with flight, like so many others before him, caused

The Library of Congress >> Exhibitions >> American Treasures

On December 17, 1903, Wilbur and Orville Wright made the world's first sustained, powered, and controlled flight in a heavier-than-air flying machine, thereby realizing one of mankind's oldest and most persistent aspirations -- human flight. *The Dream of Flight* honors that achievement, using the Library's rarest and most significant materials to explore the notion that flight, whether fanciful or actual, has inspired and occupied a central place in most cultures.

**Exhibition Sections:**

Exhibition Overview     Object List

The Dream     Public Programs

The Achievement     Read More About It

Timeline of Flight     Credits

Please fill out our online surve

Look for these "Discov spotlight items of specia

**The Dream of Flight** is an online exhibit of materials from the Library of Congress that puts the Wrights' achievements in a broader context. It examines the history of manned flight by looking at myth and religion, winged features, and earlier technologies such as dirigibles.

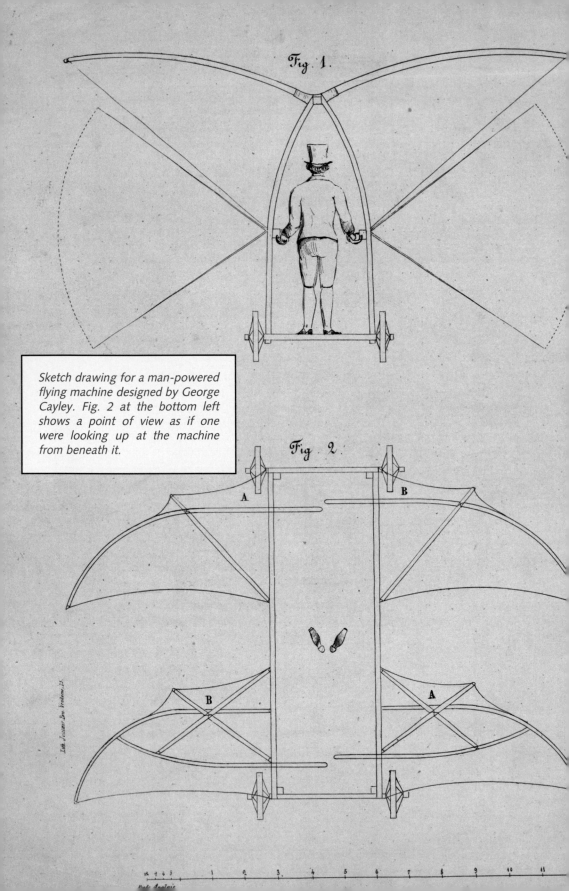

Fig. 1.

Fig. 2.

A          B

B          A

*Sketch drawing for a man-powered flying machine designed by George Cayley. Fig. 2 at the bottom left shows a point of view as if one were looking up at the machine from beneath it.*

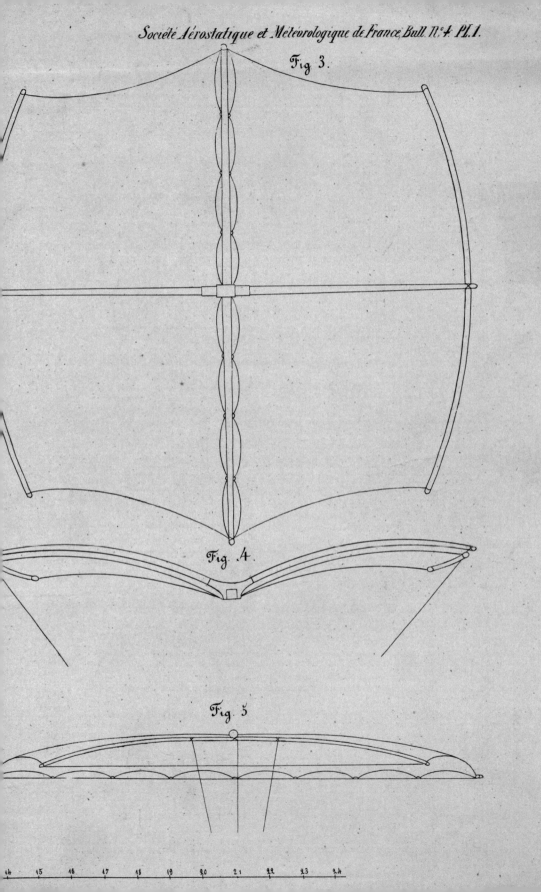

Fig 3.

Fig. 4.

Fig. 5.

him to study aerodynamics. In 1796, he created the first model helicopter with contra-rotating propellers. This design has two propellers, with one placed behind the other, which can produce a lot of power.

In 1804, Cayley invented a model monoplane air glider, which looks much like modern-day airplanes. He then discovered that dihedral (wings set lower at their center and higher at their outer ends) improved lateral stability. He continued his research using models and by 1807 had come to understand that a curved lifting surface generated

This **George Cayley** Web page provides an illustrated introduction to Sir George Cayley, an important figure in early aviation and author of the 1810 work *On Aerial Navigation.*

more lift than a flat surface of equal area. By 1810 Cayley had published his three-part treatise *On Aerial Navigation*. This classic text stated that lift, propulsion, and control were the three essential elements to successful flight. Cayley was apparently the first person to realize and state this.[2]

In 1849, Cayley devised a flying machine, much like his original air glider. He sat a ten-year-old boy in it for at least one short flight. A year later, with a bigger model, he asked his coachman to be the pilot. The story is that the coachman replied that he had been hired to drive a coach, not to fly a glider![3]

## ⊜ THE AGE OF AVIATION

Cayley's ideas and inventions only continued to spur the imagination of other inventors and scientists. The age of aviation was opening up. Ideas from scientists and inventors such as William S. Henson and John Stringfellow flowed, and the race was on. Who would build the first flying machine and keep it in the air? Henson wanted to create a flying machine that would carry a human.

He called it the Aerial Steam Carriage and developed the Aerial Transit Company to produce the planes. It never happened. When testing the model, it failed. It was also very expensive. Henson moved to the United States with his family and never talked about aviation again.

Stringfellow, who worked with William Henson, continued pursuing his dream to fly. In 1868, he created the steam-powered triplane. This was the very first flying machine to have a steam engine and stay aloft. The steam engine won first prize at the Crystal Palace Exhibition in London. Today it is on display in the Early Flight Gallery of the National Air and Space Museum in Washington, D.C.

By the early twentieth century, aviation was the new frontier. Inventors in Europe and the United States, including Orville and Wilbur Wright, were trying to conquer flight. Originally,

Airplanes Inventors: Otto Lilienthal - Microsoft Internet Explorer

File   Edit   View   Favorites   Tools   Help

Address http://www.wright-house.com/wright-brothers/inventors/Lilienthal.html

# Otto Lilienthal

## (1848-1896)

If Cayley is aviation's grandfather, Otto Lilienthal is its uncle. From statements and writings left by the Wright brothers, it is clear Lilienthal was an important source of inspiration for their efforts. A case can be made that the writings of Lilienthal directly inspired the Wrights to take on the invention of the airplane as an interesting pursuit. Certainly their early framing of the "problem of flight" was derived largely from Lilienthal's ideas and difficulties. Echoes from Lilienthal's article *Practical Experiments for the Development of Human Flight* are clearly evident in Wilbur's address to the Western Society of Engineers, and in his first letter to Octave Chanute.

Before 1881, attempts to develop airplanes and gliders were occasional and sporadic. Lilienthal changed all that. Indeed, Lilienthal's efforts broke the 'respectability barrier' that haunted serious efforts to develop airplanes. Before Lilienthal, building a heavier-than-air craft was widely considered to be the province of dreamers and fools; afterwords it seemed possible to fly. Thus ____ the beginning of the experimental period of active research on heavier-than-air flight. Lilienthal de____ erent models of his gliders over a span of 5 years. His efforts received worldwide publicity, and his ____ courage to follow in his footsteps.

F____ ers were monoplanes, three were biplanes. Each model was a hang glider, controlled by the pilot sh____ than through the use of any active control surfaces. These eighteen craft will be described separately at some ____ efully-not-too-distant future.

Sir Cha____

Done

This site provides a brief biography of **Otto Lilienthal,** an important figure in the early history of aviation whose work influenced the Wrights.

man wanted to fly like the birds. Gliders were invented. German engineer Otto Lilienthal studied aerodynamics and worked to design a glider that would fly. Otto Lilienthal was the first person to design a glider that could hold a person and had the ability to fly long distances. Wilbur Wright in particular read his findings in a paper Lilienthal wrote called *The Problem of Flying and Practical Experiments in Soaring.*

## → LANGLEY AND CHANUTE

At about the same time, Samuel Langley was granted fifty thousand dollars to build a glider with power. He realized that man needed power to fly any distance. He built a steam-motored plane he called the *Aerodrome.* Langley wrote *Experiments in Aerodynamics* and the *Aeronautical Annuals of 1895, 1896, and 1897.* These were also read by the Wright brothers with great interest.

Octave Chanute was a civil engineer inspired by Otto Lilienthal. Chanute spent much of his life designing several aircraft. His most popular model was the Herring-Chanute Biplane. He published his studies called *Progress in Flying Machines* in 1894. The Wright brothers used this book for many of their experiments. Chanute also experimented with gliders in Indiana. Chanute was a forefather to the Wrights, and in fact, he became good friends with the Wright brothers.

Although the businesses the Wright brothers worked at were successful in many ways, they both wanted more. They read about these great pioneers of flight. They studied their experiments. The combination of Wilbur's love of books and Orville's love of mechanics led them to become the first men to fly.

## ⇒ GLIDERS

The biplane box kite Wilbur and Orville created in Dayton, Ohio, in 1899 was a huge success. The Wrights were looking for a suitable location to fly a glider. Wilbur wrote to the U.S. Weather Bureau asking about wind predictions in the Chicago area. Wilbur told the bureau they would be flying a kite capable of sustaining a man. The Wrights not only needed a place with good winds, but also a place that had a soft landing. They changed their mind about Chicago. In August 1900, the Wrights decided that Kitty Hawk, North Carolina, would be a more suitable place.

Wilbur went to Kitty Hawk first and set up camp. It was an isolated area. There were no bridges connecting the beach with any other part of North Carolina. The town of Kitty Hawk was about a mile away from the beach and very small. Orville stayed behind to run the bicycle shop, but met Wilbur a month later at the end of September. When Orville arrived, the glider was nearly finished.

Even though the brothers were four years apart, they were inseparable. Orville wanted to be a part of the process of building and testing the glider. Even though Wilbur and Orville Wright would argue, they always felt it was the Wright brothers against the world.

▲ The Wright brothers chose Kitty Hawk, North Carolina, as the location to set up camp and build a flying machine. This photo is from 1900, and offers an accurate view of the large, isolated and open place in which the young men carried out their dreams of flight.

▲ Octave Chanute, Orville, and Edward Huffaker seated, Wilbur standing. This shed functioned as the working place where the glider was built and repaired. Next to it, the white tent served as sleeping quarters.

The glider would be able to hold a man. It was very lightweight. It was made of French sateen fabric, ash, and white pine. Originally, Wilbur wanted to use spruce, but he could not find enough lumber. He had to settle for white pine. The glider looked like a biplane but with no engine. With a man lying down in the middle, the plane weighed about 190 pounds. Unfortunately, the glider was still not strong enough to fly. Orville wrote:

> Our machine was designed to be flown as a kite, with a man on board, in winds of from fifteen to twenty miles an hour. But, upon trial, it was found that much stronger winds were required to lift it. Suitable winds not being plentiful, we found it necessary, in order to test the new balancing system, to fly the machine as a kite without a man on board, operating the levers through cords from the ground.[4]

Then, in a gust of wind, the glider was destroyed. The Wright brothers traveled back to Dayton to start over.

## A New Glider

The Wrights returned to North Carolina a year later in 1901. This time they set up camp at Kill Devil Hills. They had the design for a glider twice the size of their original. Because they had lift problems before, they were sure to follow Otto Lilienthal's calculations exactly.

Camping on the dunes at Kill Devil Hills was hard. A friend of Octave Chanute, Edward Huffaker, joined the brothers. He knew a lot about aerodynamics, but he did not help the Wrights build their glider. This made the Wrights mad. They felt Huffaker was a nuisance. He talked a lot and left valuable equipment like stopwatches out in the sand.

www.GeorgeSpratt.org - Microsoft Internet Explorer

File   Edit   View   Favorites   Tools   Help

Address http://www.georgespratt.org/

# www.GeorgeSpratt.org

*George A. Spratt and his son, George G. Spratt, with their glider in 1909.*

Two original thinkers, creators and lifelong experimenters in aviation.

Dr. Ge
experi

**George Spratt** worked with the Wrights at Kitty Hawk between 1901 and 1903. This Web site describes his contributions to manned flight and his relationship with the Wrights.

First

Done

A man named George Spratt later joined the brothers. Spratt also experimented with model gliders. He had some medical experience too, which Chanute thought was important to have, since testing gliders was very dangerous. Spratt helped at the camp and the Wrights appreciated his company. Unfortunately, the most unwelcome guests arrived by the thousands—mosquitoes! A swamp about fifty miles away produced a large number of mosquitoes. With a northwest wind, the mosquitoes found their way to the Wrights' camp. When Orville wrote to his sister, Kate, he told her, "Typhoid fever had been more pleasant . . . The sand and grass and trees and hills and everything was fairly covered with them. They chewed us clean through our underwear and 'socks,' lumps began swelling up all over my body like hens' eggs."[5]

They tried to wrap themselves up in blankets with just their noses sticking out. But then the wind stopped and the heat in the blankets was unbearable. It was impossible to work on the glider for several days. The only way to keep the mosquitoes away was to burn old tree stumps so that there was a lot of smoke. Soon, with the mosquitoes gone and the heat more tolerable, the Wrights and their visitors got back to work.

## Chanute Lends a Hand

A new visitor joined the crew. Octave Chanute went to the Wright's camp at Kill Devil Hills and helped the Wright brothers perfect their glider. One of the biggest changes the Wrights made to this glider was in the size of the wings. The new and improved glider had a wingspan of twenty-two feet (6.7 meters) with wings that were seven feet (2.1 meters) wide.[6] It was flown as both a kite and glider. But time after time, it did not fly as smoothly as the Wrights wanted it to. It was not easy to get the new glider up the dune. It only weighed ninety pounds, but sand got in their shoes and socks.

CHANUTE GLIDING EXPERIMENT

1902 - TURNING TO THE RIGHT

*Penciled at the top of the photo, it reads: Chanute gliding experiment 1902–Turning to the right. Octave Chanute, a champion of aviation, became associated with the Wright brothers in 1899, and served as their mentor until his death in 1910.*

▲ *This wooden shed was built in July 1901 to house the glider in bad weather. In this photo from August of the same year, the Wright glider is being rebuilt.*

Wilbur grabbed the bars. He was going to pilot the glider first. Orville and the other men helped to give the glider lift. They ran as hard as they could in the soft sand down the dune, but the glider nearly crashed, which left them puzzled. Their original *Flyer* worked better. Why was this not getting the lift they needed?

They kept trying. They hoisted the glider, ran down the hill, and . . . thunk! The glider landed in the sand nose down. To help keep the glider from going nose down, Wilbur changed his position over and over. He wanted the center of gravity to be toward the back of the glider. But this made it difficult to control the glider. It worked better on the ninth try. With Wilbur back as far as he could go, the glider started to climb higher and higher. This is what happened to Lilienthal's glider when it stalled in midair and crashed, killing Lilienthal. The Wrights knew this too. Orville shouted to Wilbur. Wilbur crept forward on the glider. It was hard to control. It swooped in the sky like a bird out of control!

The Wrights only continued to have problems with their glider. Each time something went wrong the Wrights had to correct it. Wilbur kept a diary and wrote down the positive and negative

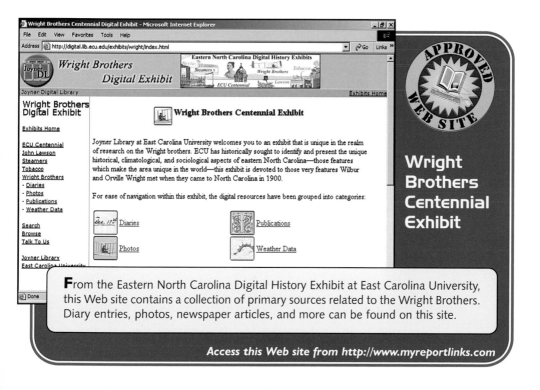

From the Eastern North Carolina Digital History Exhibit at East Carolina University, this Web site contains a collection of primary sources related to the Wright Brothers. Diary entries, photos, newspaper articles, and more can be found on this site.

*Access this Web site from http://www.myreportlinks.com*

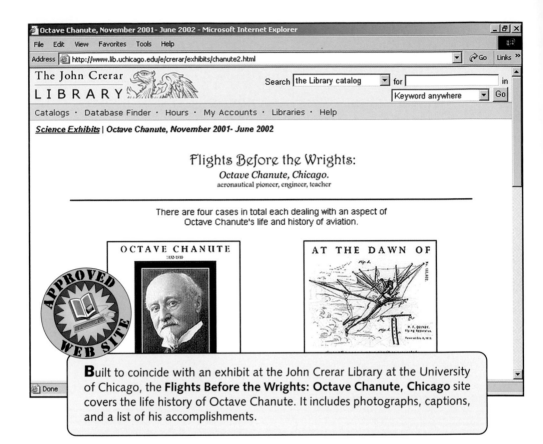

Built to coincide with an exhibit at the John Crerar Library at the University of Chicago, the **Flights Before the Wrights: Octave Chanute, Chicago** site covers the life history of Octave Chanute. It includes photographs, captions, and a list of his accomplishments.

things about the glider. On the upside, it was stronger and safer. They also resolved wing warping problems. But on the negative side, it was not lifting into the air, not as stable as their kite in 1900, and it was sluggish and uncontrollable. The Wrights rebuilt the wings, this time reducing the curve in their shape. They went with their own instincts and gave up on Lilienthal's ideas.

A week later, the Wrights tried the glider again. It was a huge success. Wilbur climbed to three hundred feet and could easily control the glider. Wilbur said, "The control of the machine seemed so good that we then felt no apprehension in sailing boldly forth. And thereafter we made glide after glide, sometimes following the ground closely, and sometimes sailing high in the air."[7]

Still, there were problems to be worked out. When rain came, the men decided to go home. In fact, Wilbur and Orville were frustrated that they had not done better. Wilbur said, "We doubted that we would ever resume our experiments. . . . When we looked at the time and money we had expended, and considered the progress made and the distance yet to go, we considered our experiments a failure."[8] Orville was sure humans would not fly for another thousand years. Just as the Wrights were feeling defeated, it was their new friend Chanute who encouraged them. He did not see failure on the dunes, but success. Chanute saw the largest glider ever created fly carrying a man.

# Gliding to Success

**T**oday, pilots and aviation experts take for granted certain principles of flight. During the Wright brothers time, these principles were not known. It was the Wright brothers, through their many experiments, who realized the connection between certain flight principles and controlling their flying machines. When they arrived back in Dayton, the brothers were both excited and a little sad. They had hoped to do more in Kill Devil Hills with their glider. Yet, they had accomplished a lot.

## PRY

Pitch, roll, and yaw (PRY) are common terms used today in aviation. Pitch is the movement the nose of an airplane makes going up or down. In today's planes, it is controlled by the elevator or the tail of an aircraft. Roll is the back and forth movement of an airplane from side to side. In modern aircraft, it is controlled by the ailerons on the wings. Yaw is the movement of an airplane's nose from side

**CHAPTER 4**

to side. It is controlled by the rudder.[1] These terms were not known or common in the Wright brothers' day. It was important for them to not only realize these basic principles of flight, but also to apply them to their aircraft, be it a kite, glider, or powered airplane.

Many aviators at the turn of the twentieth century were not aware of these principles. This is where the Wright brothers succeeded. They realized that a flying machine needed coordinated control over all of these functions. Once this was achieved, an aircraft could safely fly.

Before they set out again with their new glider, Wilbur and Orville Wright tried other experiments. They modified a bicycle by adding a horizontal wheel directly over the front wheel. They attached to it airfoils (like wings) of different sizes and shapes and rode up and down the street. The brothers were trying to compare the effects of wind on different surfaces. The problem with this practice was that each

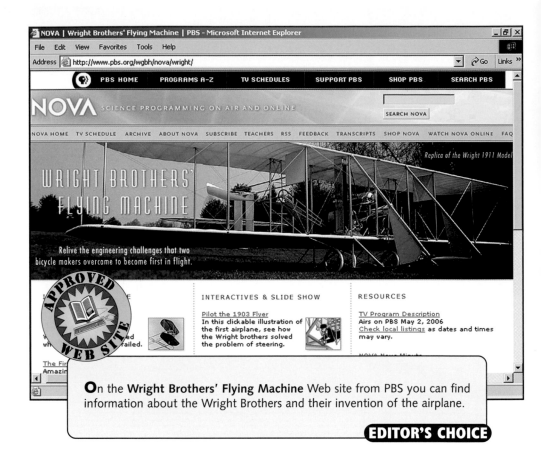

On the **Wright Brothers' Flying Machine** Web site from PBS you can find information about the Wright Brothers and their invention of the airplane.

**EDITOR'S CHOICE**

time they rode the bicycle, conditions were different. The wind might be stronger, the road bumpier, the speed of the bike faster or slower. Orville and Wilbur needed an experiment in which conditions would remain constant.

## THE WIND TUNNEL

This predicament led them to another experiment not yet done. Although wind tunnels were not a new idea, using them with aircraft designs was. "We had taken up aeronautics merely as a sport. We reluctantly entered upon the scientific side of it. But we soon found the work so fascinating that we were drawn into it deeper and deeper. Two testing-machines were built, which we believed would avoid the errors to which the measurements of others had been subject."[2]

One of the testing machines the brothers built was a wind tunnel. It was six feet long and sixteen inches square. It had a glass top so the brothers could see inside. A small engine was used to power a fan. This created the wind.

The brothers then created miniature wings and tail sections. They placed them at the end of the wind tunnel and turned on the fan. By shaping the wings in various airfoils, they were able to determine

This site describes in detail the mechanical aspects of flight. It covers topics such as the different parts of a plane and their functions, and how air travels over different types of wings.

*Access this Web site from http://www.myreportlinks.com*

how much "lift" a wing would get based on its shape.

The Wrights studied the writings of previous scientists and discovered that they were not always correct. Wilbur and Orville knew they had to find new ways to test their own theories. They experimented on their own. "To work intelligently, one needs to know the effects of a multitude of variations that could be incorporated in the surfaces of flying-machines . . . The shape of the edge also makes a difference, so that thousands of combinations are possible in so simple a thing as a wing."[3]

## ⇨ SMEATON'S COEFFICIENT

Unlike other scientists and inventors before them, the Wright brothers continually found ways to experiment. Instead of experimenting with the whole craft (kite, glider, or airplane) they found ways to experiment on individual parts of the craft such as the wings, controls, and propeller. They experimented by trial and error. This meant they tried something, saw how it worked or did not work, and based on those findings, they would make a change and try again. Trial and error was used when they flew their kites and gliders.

To perform these experiments, the Wrights used wind tunnels and a modified bicycle. They also used formulas. By plugging in a set of numbers or data, the brothers could come up with ideas or

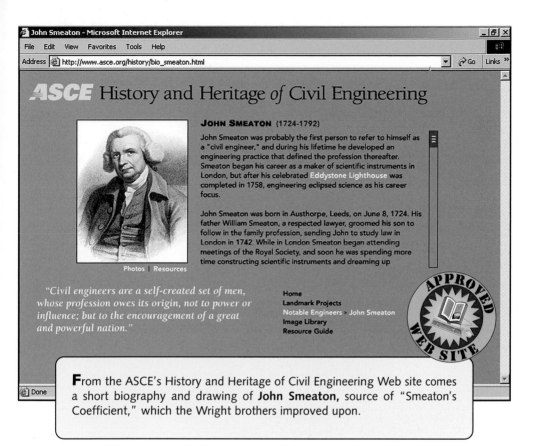

## ASCE History and Heritage of Civil Engineering

### JOHN SMEATON (1724-1792)

John Smeaton was probably the first person to refer to himself as a "civil engineer," and during his lifetime he developed an engineering practice that defined the profession thereafter. Smeaton began his career as a maker of scientific instruments in London, but after his celebrated Eddystone Lighthouse was completed in 1758, engineering eclipsed science as his career focus.

John Smeaton was born in Austhorpe, Leeds, on June 8, 1724. His father William Smeaton, a respected lawyer, groomed his son to follow in the family profession, sending John to study law in London in 1742. While in London Smeaton began attending meetings of the Royal Society, and soon he was spending more time constructing scientific instruments and dreaming up

Photos | Resources

*"Civil engineers are a self-created set of men, whose profession owes its origin, not to power or influence; but to the encouragement of a great and powerful nation."*

Home
Landmark Projects
Notable Engineers > John Smeaton
Image Library
Resource Guide

From the ASCE's History and Heritage of Civil Engineering Web site comes a short biography and drawing of **John Smeaton**, source of "Smeaton's Coefficient," which the Wright brothers improved upon.

theories on how something might work. One formula used was called Smeaton's Coefficient.

John Smeaton was a British engineer. In 1759, he wrote a paper called "An Experimental Enquiry Concerning the Natural Powers of Water and Wind to Turn Mills and Other Machines Depending on Circular Motion." Smeaton talked about how moving objects in the air were affected by pressure and velocity. He came up with a formula that was believed to be right for 150 more years. That was until the Wright brothers came along. They used Smeaton's formula to figure out how much lift and

Positioned on his stomach in the small space cut out in the middle of the lower wing, Wilbur Wright manages the controls as the 1902 glider soars over the beach of Kitty Hawk, North Carolina.

drag an object would have. This formula used the number .005 to determine the "pressure factor." However, the Wright brothers soon realized that this was wrong. When they built their glider based on this factor, it did not get enough lift. The glider would not stay afloat for very long.

With the wind tunnel experiments, the brothers took Smeaton's coefficient and tested individual wings. For over a hundred years, great scientists and inventors including Otto Lilienthal used Smeaton's coefficient. It had to be right!  Soon, the Wrights realized that Smeaton's coefficient for lift should not be .005, but .0033. This realization was huge for the aviation community. With the new and correct number, the Wrights were able to develop better wings. In total, they conducted hundreds of experiments using the wind tunnel.

## ⮕ THE HANGAR

In late August, the Wrights headed back to Kitty Hawk. This time they had a new and improved glider. It was even bigger than the last one—32 feet long. It was also the biggest flying machine ever built. After many wind tunnel tests, they had decided that long narrow wings were the best way to go.

The Wright brothers lived in a wooden building called a hangar, which also housed the 1902 glider. They built the hangar themselves. Although it was very cramped, Orville and Wilbur did not care. They loved being at Kitty Hawk with their flying machines. Orville loved the idea of flying so much that it was what made him happiest. He wrote, "Wilbur and I could hardly wait for morning to come to get at something that interested us. That's happiness!"[4]

## 1902 Glider

The brothers also added a hip cradle to their glider. This new control operated the warping mechanism of the wings. Even though it had its share of problems, it was the most advanced system in the world.[5] They also added a double vertical tail to add stability. Orville wrote, "We are convinced that the trouble with the 1901 machine is overcome by the vertical tail."[6]

For almost a month, Orville and Wilbur tested their new glider. They had some problems too. For example, it seemed the new controls might make it harder to fly the glider. One day, while Orville was piloting the glider, he moved the new hip cradle correctly, but did not put the front elevator down. The glider shot upward. Then it dashed toward the ground. There was nothing Orville could do, so the glider crashed. Fortunately, Orville was not hurt. But the elevator was badly damaged. The glider was not safe to fly.

Frustrated, the brothers debated over what the problem could be. They had added a double vertical

As Wilbur makes a right turn, notice how close the right wing is tipped to the ground. This rear-view shot was captured on October 24, 1902.

tail, but whether it was double or single did not seem to make much of a difference.

Orville went to bed that night but could not sleep. He spent the night thinking. In the morning, he had a solution. The vertical tails should not be fixed; they should be movable. This meant another control for the pilot, which the brothers wanted to avoid. So they devised a control that would operate both the steering and the rudder. When the pilot turned or banked the craft, the rudder would also turn at the same time. The brothers changed the double vertical tail to a single tail and added the new control. It seemed to work. They flew about a thousand flights. Both brothers became skilled pilots.

On October 23, 1902, Wilbur glided for 26 seconds and over 622 feet. Orville wrote, "We now hold all the records! The largest machine . . . the longest time in the air, the smallest angle of descent, and the highest wind!"[7]

# BIRTH OF THE AIRPLANE

**W**ilbur and Orville Wright returned to Dayton. They were excited that the tests on their glider had gone so well. Now the brothers had visions of building a powered airplane, one that could not only fly a man, but would also someday be useful. Wilbur wrote to George Spratt on December 29, 1902, "We are thinking of building a machine next year with 500 square feet surface. If all goes well the next step will be to apply a motor."[1]

## THE RACE TOWARD POWERED FLIGHT

The Wright brothers were not the only ones dreaming of powered flight. Aviators in Europe were also testing gliders. At this time, Paris was considered the aviation capital of the world. Yet, many of the aircraft being built were not as advanced as the Wrights' glider. Still, a Frenchman named Ferdinand Ferber was already experimenting using a glider based on the Wrights' plans.

Wilbur and Orville Wright knew the race was on. Who would be the first to fly a powered airplane? One of their

CHAPTER

5

fiercest rivals was a well-known man named Samuel Langley. He was also the secretary of the Smithsonian Institution. He knew what the Wright brothers were doing. He too had been fascinated with flight since the 1890s. Langley, however, was well funded. The Wright brothers were not. The U.S. War Department had given Langley fifty thousand dollars to build a powered airplane, which he called the *Aerodrome.*

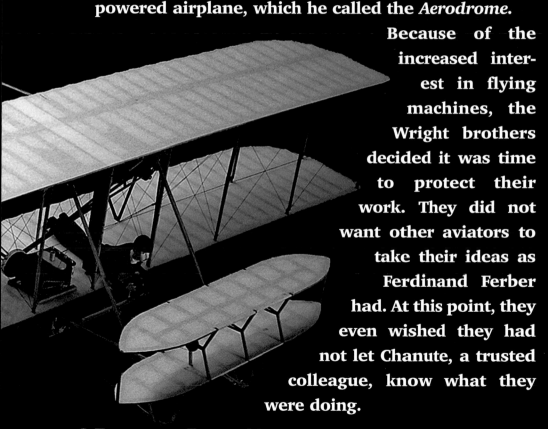

Because of the increased interest in flying machines, the Wright brothers decided it was time to protect their work. They did not want other aviators to take their ideas as Ferdinand Ferber had. At this point, they even wished they had not let Chanute, a trusted colleague, know what they were doing.

## BUILDING A FLYING MACHINE

Back in Dayton, the brothers got started on building their bigger flying machine. The first thing they needed was a strong engine. They asked several

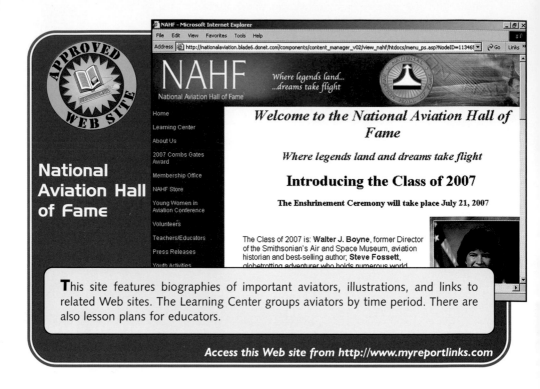

APPROVED WEB SITE

National Aviation Hall of Fame

This site features biographies of important aviators, illustrations, and links to related Web sites. The Learning Center groups aviators by time period. There are also lesson plans for educators.

**Access this Web site from http://www.myreportlinks.com**

people in the automobile industry if they would provide them with a gasoline engine. All said they were too busy making automobiles. Also, no automobile company wanted to be a part of the "crazy scheme" of having one of their engines in a flying machine.

This rejection did not deter the brothers. Instead, they decided to build their own engine. Charles Taylor, who ran the Wright brothers' bicycle shop, loaned a helping hand. First, they built a skeleton of the engine. This way, they could test it and make sure all the parts ran smoothly. When this was successful, they finished making the engine. In February 1903, they brought it into the shop for a test run. It did not work at all. It was not until May that they had a running engine.

Meanwhile, outside pressure built. News that Langley was going to test his *Aerodrome* reached the Wrights while they were in the process of building the body of the *Flyer*. They made the wings longer. This flying machine would be the largest ever built.

Sure enough, a problem arose. There was an unexpected issue with the propellers. For years, propellers had been used on boats and balloons,

A rear-view shot of the four-cylinder motor as that was installed in the Wright brothers' 1903 glider. The pilot would lie on his stomach in the seat to the left.

but never on a flying machine. Stumped for ideas and low on money, the brothers decided to create their own propeller. The brothers learned about propellers and theorized how they would work on paper. They had to be accurate. A propeller is a rotating airfoil. The Wrights figured that a propeller is shaped much like a wing. "Like a wing, it creates a difference in pressure, more on the back of the blade than on the front."[2]

## FIGURING OUT THE PROPELLER

The Wright brothers argued often about the propeller. They were frustrated. Orville said, "Often after an hour or so of heated argument, we would discover that we were as far from agreement as when we started, but that each had changed to the other's original position."[3] The more time and effort they put into creating a propeller that would work for their flying machine, the more they realized they did not know. After several months, what they discovered was amazing. They realized that it was better to use two large propellers that rotated slowly rather than one large propeller that rotated quickly. The propellers would rotate toward each other, which would reduce torque. Torque is a turning or twisting force. Amazingly, this idea would not be rediscovered until 1930.

They carved the first propeller from a solid block of wood using a hatchet and a draw knife. Then they tested it on a two horsepower engine. It worked well, but this was just a test propeller. The actual propellers used on their airplane would be made of spruce and then covered in a lightweight canvas.

The airplane was finally coming together. Soon it would be time to test it.

## ⇒THE COMPETITION

In the meantime, progress was being made by Langley. He had developed what he thought would be the first powered flying machine. He had a lot of money to spend, too. People had high

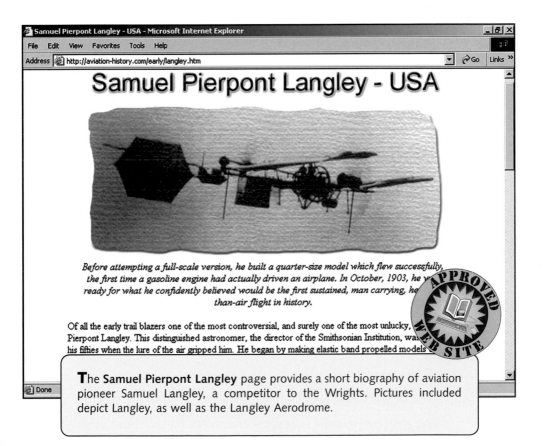

Samuel Pierpont Langley - USA - Microsoft Internet Explorer

Address http://aviation-history.com/early/langley.htm

# Samuel Pierpont Langley - USA

*Before attempting a full-scale version, he built a quarter-size model which flew successfully, the first time a gasoline engine had actually driven an airplane. In October, 1903, he was ready for what he confidently believed would be the first sustained, man carrying, heavier-than-air flight in history.*

Of all the early trail blazers one of the most controversial, and surely one of the most unlucky, was Pierpont Langley. This distinguished astronomer, the director of the Smithsonian Institution, was in his fifties when the lure of the air gripped him. He began by making elastic band propelled models

**The Samuel Pierpont Langley** page provides a short biography of aviation pioneer Samuel Langley, a competitor to the Wrights. Pictures included depict Langley, as well as the Langley Aerodrome.

hopes that Langley would build the first airplane. Like the Wright brothers, he had studied aerodynamics and flight.

On October 7, 1903, while the Wrights were still building their airplane, Langley attempted his first manned flight. Charles Manley was the pilot. Langley had many problems getting the flying machine ready for this big day. Langley built a houseboat on the Potomac River. On top of the houseboat was a track. This was where his flying machine would launch. It was quite a sight! The flying machine looked funny to many of the reporters. The press was there to watch and capture this amazing event on film. Most were certain that Langley would be the first man to build a flying machine able to carry man.

## Plop!

It was a breezy day, and Charles Manley was anxious to get this machine in the air. The engine was started. The propellers whirred. The great *Aerodrome* quickly raced down the track. Plop! It landed headfirst into the cold Potomac River. Was the pilot alive? As people raced to the wreckage, they saw Manley scrambling to get away from it. Photos were taken of the event. One newspaper reporter said, "[The machine flew like] a handful of mortar."[4]

Langley did not surrender his dream to fly. The Wrights were still working on their flying machine and were not able to test it yet. The *Aerodrome* was rescued and repaired and a second flight was tried. Charles Manley climbed into the machine, started the engine, and got ready to fly. As the *Aerodrome* raced down the track, it took to the air. Could this be happening? Could Manley really be flying? Suddenly, without warning, the mighty *Aerodrome* broke into two pieces. It fell into the Potomac River. Charles Manley again scrambled to safety. It was the end for Langley, who decided to retire.

As it turned out, the wings on Langley's *Aerodrome* could not support the weight of the flying

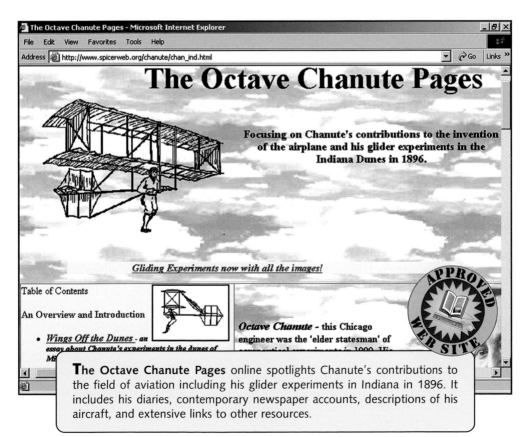

The **Octave Chanute Pages** online spotlights Chanute's contributions to the field of aviation including his glider experiments in Indiana in 1896. It includes his diaries, contemporary newspaper accounts, descriptions of his aircraft, and extensive links to other resources.

machine. The part of the wing that carried most of the weight did not have the support it needed. It broke apart as soon as the machine was in the air. Langley did not realize this—nor did anyone else—until the Wrights experimented with their wind tunnels.

Later, Wilbur Wright wrote to Octave Chanute, "I see that Langley has had his fling, and failed. It seems to be our turn to throw now, and I wonder what our luck will be."[5]

## BACK TO KILL DEVIL HILLS

Wilbur and Orville arrived at Kill Devil Hills on August 28. Things seemed to be in good order, and the 1902 glider was not damaged. Orville hoped to have it up in the air for experiments shortly. With their new set of controls, they were able to fly the glider well.

The Wrights got busy assembling their new and much larger flying machine, called the *Wright Flyer*. The 12 horsepower aluminum engine they built weighed 170 pounds (77.1 kilograms), which brought the total weight of the airship to about 750 pounds (340.2 kilograms). With the weight of the pilot, that was almost 70 pounds (31.75 kilograms) more than they had calculated. The question remained: Could the propellers they designed produce enough thrust to get the machine in the air?

A second question came up. How would the flying machine be launched? If they added wheels, that would increase the weight. It would also cause the machine to sink in the sand. The Wrights, along with the help of George Spratt, laid out a long track. They attached the flying machine to a truck that would carry it down the track.

On November 4, 1903, the flying machine was ready to be tested. But as the Wrights started the engine, it huffed and puffed. Then it quit. Both the propellers broke off and damaged the shafts. It was a frustrating time because the brothers knew

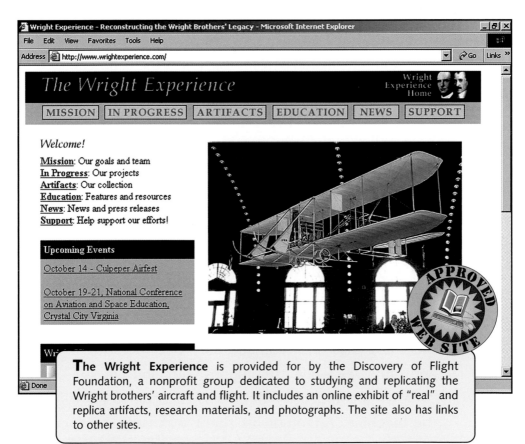

The Wright Experience is provided for by the Discovery of Flight Foundation, a nonprofit group dedicated to studying and replicating the Wright brothers' aircraft and flight. It includes an online exhibit of "real" and replica artifacts, research materials, and photographs. The site also has links to other sites.

it would take weeks to repair the shafts, and the weather was getting colder as the winter approached.

On November 20, the new shafts arrived from Dayton and were quickly attached to the flying machine. The Wrights did not give up despite the fact that one problem after another occurred. The engine was not getting the fuel it needed. The brothers fixed it. The propeller had a hairline crack. The brothers fixed it. The weather was not cooperating. Storms rolled onshore making it difficult to do anything. They could not fix the weather—only wait for it to get better, and it did.

Finally, on December 13, with a mild breeze, the weather seemed perfect to fly. But the brothers did not. Instead, they spent the day reading and walking along the beach. It was Sunday and they were not going to break the Sabbath just to fly .their machine.

## ⮕ Success!

Monday, December 14, was a good day. People were asked to come to watch the event. The Wrights wanted many witnesses. But only a few people showed up. Five men from the nearby life-saving station arrived to help. Two small boys and their dog also showed, but they became scared and ran away when the engines were started.

After a coin toss, Wilbur was the first to pilot the machine. Although his flight was very short, he was flying! The *Flyer* did not last long in the air and landed hard. One of the front skids broke in the sand. It was soon fixed.

December 17 was a cold and angry day. It was windy and the sky looked like it was going to storm. The brothers hurried to get the plane on the track and into the air. This time Orville was the pilot. The flying machine sailed down the track at six miles an hour. Minutes later it was airborne! Then it landed gently on the sand. The flight lasted twelve seconds and the flying machine flew 120 feet. Success was theirs—the Wrights were the first to fly.

# AGE OF FLIGHT

**T**he Wright brothers flew three more times that day. They were very happy. They knew they had achieved their dream to fly. They were eager to get home and celebrate Christmas with their family.

Even though they had success, many problems and troubles lay ahead. Because there were not many people there to witness this great event, many people speculated as to what happened. Newspaper writers either wrote too much or did not say enough, and rarely did they get the information right. The Wrights did not receive much respect. Many people still thought that flying was a crazy idea.

**CHAPTER**

**6**

## BACK AT DAYTON

In 1904, the Wrights decided to stay in Dayton, Ohio. They built a shed in a farmer's field at Huffman Prairie. Wilbur wrote to Octave Chanute on June 21, 1904, "We are in a large meadow . . . In addition to cattle there have been a dozen or more horses in the pasture...and we have been at much trouble to get them safely away before making trials."[1]

Still, it did not deter the Wrights. Now that they had a flying machine, it was time to make it practical. This meant that they needed to make it safe and useful.

The Wrights also wanted to protect their invention from mischievous eyes. The trolley track ran by the pasture and shed where the Wrights kept their airplane. They knew the trolley's schedule though. After the trolley passed with its curious passengers, the Wrights would pull the airplane out of the shed, work on it, and then hide it again before the next trolley passed.

The brothers worked hard making changes to their original *Flyer*. They built two engines and changed the airfoil section. On testing day, they invited people, including their father, to watch. The new and improved flying machine barely got off the ground. The Wrights continued to work on their plane throughout the summer. Lack of winds did not help. Neither did the warmer weather. They built a cata-pult. It was a tall tower with weights attached to a cable. When they released the weights, the cable shot the *Flyer* into the air. The idea was similar to the catapults later used on aircraft carriers. The catapults launch jets into the air because the runway is so short.

Finally, on December 1, 1904, Orville flew the airplane for five minutes. Apparently, the cooler air made all the difference. The engine produced more power in the cooler air. In 1904, the Wrights made over a hundred flights.

## ⇒ TIME FOR REWARDS

The Wrights were happy with the new *Flyer II*. They had spent many years and a lot of their own money building the flying machine. Now it showed great potential to be a useful airplane. The Wrights wanted to approach the U.S. War Department. They wanted the United States to have the first opportunity to buy their airplane. The French government wanted to buy the *Flyer* for the French Army. They were going to buy the airplane for $200,000 but that deal did not happen. Wilbur wrote to his congressman, "It not only flies through the air at high speed, but also lands without being wrecked."[2]

The response from the United States government was not good. They told the Wrights that the government wanted a practical airplane, and would not be interested until the Wrights had produced this. However, this is exactly what the Wright brothers had done.

The Wrights continued to make changes to the *Flyer* in 1905. They also encountered more problems. Orville even crashed the plane on July 14, 1905. He had made a controlled turn, but had problems with the pitch. The nose of the *Flyer* turned down and crashed at 30 miles per hour. Orville was all right, but the Wrights had to make steering easier. They made the vertical rudder bigger. This seemed to help.

In September 1905, the *Flyer* became the first practical airplane. It had separate pitch, yaw, and roll controls. The Wrights flew it all the time. They

Orville and Wilbur stand with their Wright Flyer 2 at Huffman Prairie near Dayton, Ohio.

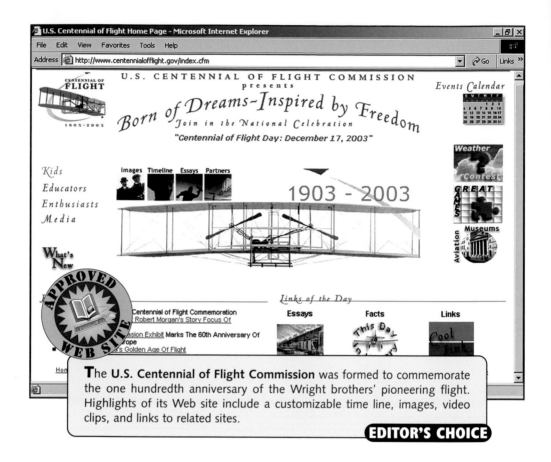

U.S. Centennial of Flight Home Page - Microsoft Internet Explorer

File   Edit   View   Favorites   Tools   Help

Address http://www.centennialofflight.gov/index.cfm            Go   Links »

CENTENNIAL OF
FLIGHT

U.S. CENTENNIAL OF FLIGHT COMMISSION
presents

Born of Dreams~Inspired by Freedom
Join in the National Celebration
"Centennial of Flight Day: December 17, 2003"

Events Calendar

1903 - 2003

Kids
Educators
Enthusiasts
Media

Images  Timeline  Essays  Partners

Weather

GREAT

Museums

What's
New

Links of the Day

Centennial of Flight Commemoration
Robert Morgan's Story Focus Of
...sion Exhibit Marks The 60th Anniversary Of
...rope
...'s Golden Age Of Flight

Essays

Facts

Links

The **U.S. Centennial of Flight Commission** was formed to commemorate the one hundredth anniversary of the Wright brothers' pioneering flight. Highlights of its Web site include a customizable time line, images, video clips, and links to related sites.

**EDITOR'S CHOICE**

could maneuver it easily and land smoothly. Many people in the Dayton area watched as the Wrights flew. The Wrights felt they could make some money from the *Flyer.* The United States government still would not give them a patent. To protect their invention, the Wrights took the *Flyer* apart and stored it. They did not fly for two and half years.

Even though the Wright brothers had applied for a patent from the U.S. Patents Office ten months before their 1903 *Flyer* flew, the office did not grant the patent until 1906. Today, the scientific principles used in the patent are still used for airplanes.

## ⊛ FLYING OVERSEAS

Despite the patent, the United States government still did not seem interested. The Wrights took their idea to Europe. They contacted the governments of France, England, Russia, and Germany to see if any would be interested in buying their flying machine. They were turned down. After all, how could two bicycle repairmen invent an airplane? The Wrights did not give up. They believed in their *Flyer,* and they knew it could change the world. They, modified it by adding a second seat and a stronger engine.

In 1907, the U.S. Army Signal Corps, part of which would later become the United States Air Force, decided to look at the flying machine. Then

In 1905, the glider was remodeled to include pilot and passenger seats. This image of the remodeled machine was taken in 1908.

shortly after, France showed great interest. For the first time, Wilbur and Orville went their own ways. Wilbur went to France and Orville traveled to Virginia.

Wilbur sailed along with the *Flyer* to France. Negotiations would be long and hard. The *Flyer* sat in the crate for a year. Interest in flying machines was greater in France, and many considered France to be the center of aviation. Finally, in 1908, Wilbur was able to show the *Flyer* to France.

## ⊜ FRANCE AND THE FLYER

Once a suitable place was found to fly the airplane, Wilbur got to work putting it together. He encountered more problems, including a serious accident. His left arm was scalded with hot water. Although he did not stop working, the problems brought delays. The French reporters criticized Wilbur and called him a "bluffer!" They did not think he could put the *Flyer* together, let alone fly it.

On a warm August day in 1908, Wilbur proved the French wrong. He was dressed in a business suit and cap, and looked a bit odd to onlookers. Wilbur started the *Flyer.* It rumbled down the track and took flight. Wilbur maneuvered the airplane with ease. He circled the field and landed the *Flyer* on the grassy ground. The crowd cheered. Wilbur had won their hearts.

Wilbur was most critical of himself. He replied to a newspaper report that he had made ten mistakes

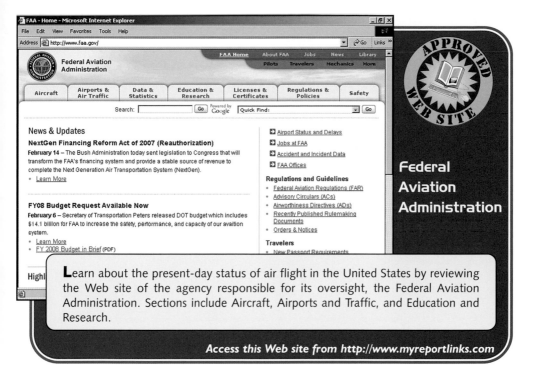

FAA - Home - Microsoft Internet Explorer

File   Edit   View   Favorites   Tools   Help

Address http://www.faa.gov/

**Federal Aviation Administration**

FAA Home    About FAA    Jobs    News    Library

Pilots    Travelers    Mechanics    More

Aircraft | Airports & Air Traffic | Data & Statistics | Education & Research | Licenses & Certificates | Regulations & Policies | Safety

Search:         Go   Powered by Google   Quick Find:         Go

**News & Updates**

**NextGen Financing Reform Act of 2007 (Reauthorization)**

**February 14** – The Bush Administration today sent legislation to Congress that will transform the FAA's financing system and provide a stable source of revenue to complete the Next Generation Air Transportation System (NextGen).

• Learn More

**FY08 Budget Request Available Now**

**February 6** – Secretary of Transportation Peters released DOT budget which includes $14.1 billion for FAA to increase the safety, performance, and capacity of our avaition system.

• Learn More
• FY 2008 Budget in Brief (PDF)

➡ Airport Status and Delays
➡ Jobs at FAA
➡ Accident and Incident Data
➡ FAA Offices

**Regulations and Guidelines**
• Federal Aviation Regulations (FAR)
• Advisory Circulars (ACs)
• Airworthiness Directives (ADs)
• Recently Published Rulemaking Documents
• Orders & Notices

**Travelers**
• New Passport Requirements

**APPROVED WEB SITE**

**Federal Aviation Administration**

Learn about the present-day status of air flight in the United States by reviewing the Web site of the agency responsible for its oversight, the Federal Aviation Administration. Sections include Aircraft, Airports and Traffic, and Education and Research.

*Access this Web site from http://www.myreportlinks.com*

while flying but was able to correct them quickly. A French newspaper, *Le Journal,* reported, "It was the first trial of the Wright airplane, whose qualities have long been regarded with doubt, and it was perfect."[3]

Wilbur continued to fly throughout August. Wilbur Wright was a hero in the eyes of French society. Postcards and souvenirs were made in his honor. It became fashionable to take a trip to the airfield and hangar where Wilbur lived and worked just to watch him fly. Wilbur wrote, "The excitement aroused by the short flights . . . is almost beyond comprehension. The French have simply become wild. Instead of doubting that we

*Katherine Wright, sister of Orville and Wilbur, sits aboard the Wright Model HS airplane, wearing a leather jacket, cap, and goggles.*

could do anything they are ready to believe we can do everything."[4]

Not only was Wilbur flying above France on a regular basis, but he also started taking passengers with him, too. On October 7, 1908, the first woman to fly was Edith O. Berg. Her husband, Hart O. Berg, flew with Wilbur first. She had to try it too. But, they had to tie up her skirts to keep them from blowing open. It is believed to have started a new skirt style in France called the Hobble skirt. Fashion designer Paul Poiret is said to have been inspired by Mrs. Berg's tied-up skirt.

People lined up to watch Wilbur fly. With all the attention Wilbur was causing, a contract was soon signed between the Wright brothers and the French.

This photograph was taken just after the Wright airplane piloted by Orville struck the ground from 75 feet (22.86 meters) up in the sky. Moments before, one of the nine-foot propeller blades broke, causing the machine to pitch to the ground. Lieutenant Selfidge was killed in the crash.

# ⇒ FORT MYER

While Wilbur was in France, Orville was busy showing the U.S. Army Signal Corps the new *Flyer*. He had to do a number of tests to show that the *Flyer* was stable and reliable, and could fly a distance. It was not easy. Sometimes the weather kept him from flying. Onlookers were not happy. They began to doubt Orville and his great flying machine.

Finally, Orville got the *Flyer* into the air, much to the crowd's delight. He flew over Arlington Cemetery in Virginia. On his return to base, he got confused with the new controls. Suddenly he was headed straight for a tent. Instead of crashing into it, he brought the *Flyer* down, causing some minor damage.

To fulfill the contract with the U.S. government, Orville had to fly with a passenger. The first airplane fatality happened on September 17, 1908. Orville was to take Lieutenant Thomas E. Selfridge up with him in the *Flyer*. He was the heaviest passenger Orville had ever flown, weighing 175 pounds. They took off and climbed into the air. It was a good flight and Selfridge seemed to be enjoying himself. Suddenly, Orville heard a loud clanking sound and decided to land. Something flew from the airplane and spun to the ground. As hard as Orville tried, he could not regain control. The *Flyer* crashed. Lieutenant Selfridge died from

On July 27, 1909, Orville Wright piloted a world record flight at Fort Myer, Virginia. The plane flew a distance of fifty miles at a speed of about forty miles an hour. Lieutenant Lahm of the U.S. Signal Corps was the passenger.

his injuries. Orville broke his leg. It took some time for Orville to recover from his injury and to get the *Flyer* repaired. Once both were better, the tests and trials began again.

Wilbur received word of the accident via telegram. He wrote in a letter to his sister Katharine, "I cannot help thinking over and over again, 'if I had been there, it would not have happened.' The worry over leaving Orville alone to undertake those trials was one of the chief things in almost breaking me down a few weeks ago and

This Web site from *Time* magazine presents the one hundred most influential people of the twentieth century. At the **TIME 100: The Wright Brothers** Web page you can read a profile of the Wright Brothers and learn about their accomplishments.

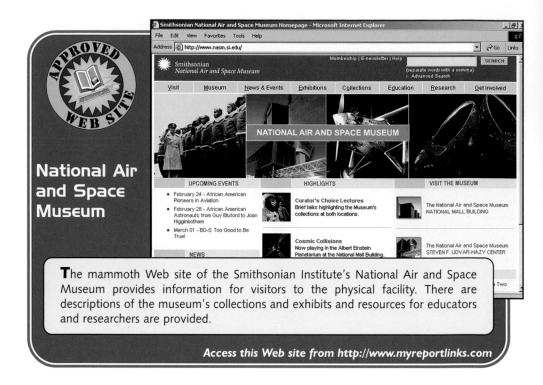

Smithsonian
*National Air and Space Museum*

Membership | E-newsletter | Help

(separate words with a comma)
▷ Advanced Search

SEARCH

| Visit | Museum | News & Events | Exhibitions | Collections | Education | Research | Get Involved |

NATIONAL AIR AND SPACE MUSEUM

UPCOMING EVENTS

- February 24 - African American Pioneers in Aviation
- February 28 - African American Astronauts from Guy Bluford to Joan Higginbotham
- March 01 - BD-5: Too Good to Be True!

NEWS

HIGHLIGHTS

**Curator's Choice Lectures**
Brief talks highlighting the Museum's collections at both locations.

**Cosmic Collisions**
Now playing in the Albert Einstein Planetarium at the National Mall Building.

VISIT THE MUSEUM

The National Air and Space Museum
NATIONAL MALL BUILDING

The National Air and Space Museum
STEVEN F. UDVAR-HAZY CENTER

**National Air and Space Museum**

**T**he mammoth Web site of the Smithsonian Institute's National Air and Space Museum provides information for visitors to the physical facility. There are descriptions of the museum's collections and exhibits and resources for educators and researchers are provided.

*Access this Web site from http://www.myreportlinks.com*

as soon as I heard the reassuring news from America I was well again."[5]

On July 2, 1909, Orville took off again and circled for eight minutes. But, as he came in for a landing, his engine stopped and the *Flyer* hit the top of a small tree. He crashed to the ground. Luckily, Orville was not injured. But repairs had to be made, delaying the tests even more.

The contract with the U.S. Signal Corps said that the Wrights had to complete a ten-mile cross-country flight. It would be the first cross-country flight in the United States. Orville and passenger Ben Foulois flew to Alexandria, Virginia, which was five miles away and back. Foulois was experienced in reading maps and would be able to assist Orville. They took off and made the flight without problems. When they returned, the crowd cheered and the U.S. War Department paid the Wrights thirty thousand dollars for the airplane.

## ➡ THE WRIGHT COMPANY

Things were going very well for the Wright brothers. Not only had Wilbur won the hearts of the French, but Orville had also sealed a deal with the United States government. Germany and Italy also wanted the Wright brothers to perform flights in their country. The Wrights' airplanes were flown in Italy, and Wilbur and Orville trained Italian pilots to fly the Wright *Flyer*.

When the Wrights returned to the United States, they came back as heroes. On June 17, 1909, all the factories in Dayton blew their whistles. All the bells rang at nine o'clock in the morning to honor the Wrights. It lasted ten minutes. A parade and fireworks were held in their honor, and the brothers received medals from the United States Congress.

Aviation companies had been started in France and Germany, but American businesspeople were slow to act. A young man named Clinton R. Peterkin approached Wilbur with an idea to start a flying-machine company. He was only twenty-four years old, but he had some connections with prominent businessmen. They bought stock in the Wrights'

This photograph taken in 1909 captures Wilbur Wright's thoughtful nature. Although not very talkative, Wilbur was an eloquent speaker and writer. It is unfortunate that his early death came at a time when the airplane was beginning to make great advances.

new company called the Wright Company. It was incorporated on November 22, 1909. They set up an office in New York City but kept the factory in Dayton, Ohio.

The Wrights built airplanes at their new company. They were very successful since airplanes were new and many people loved to watch them fly. The Wrights were making money and decided to build a new home in the suburbs. Orville also started a flying school at Huffman Field, but the first American pilots were trained here by Orville. The Wrights also continued to test new devices and fly.

## ⇒ WILBUR DIES

At first, family and friends were not terribly concerned that Wilbur was ill. He had been traveling to Europe and settling lawsuits—some people and companies were using the Wrights' ideas without permission. Wilbur was under a lot of stress. His family thought he was sick because of the stress. However, soon after he became ill, he was diagnosed with typhoid fever. This illness was somewhat common at the turn of the twentieth century, but not much was known about it. It is caused by a bacteria found in food or water tainted with feces from an infected person. The Wright family hired the best doctors to treat and care for Wilbur. Sadly, on May 30, 1912, Wilbur died. He was only forty-five years old.

*A close-up view of what the Wright airplane had evolved into by 1911. Yet this was only the beginning for the world of aviation.*

Orville was very sad. He said, "The death of my brother Wilbur is a thing we must definitely charge to our long struggle . . . The delays were what worried him to his death . . . first into a state of chronic nervousness, and then into physical fatigue which made him an easy prey for the attack of typhoid that caused his death."[6] Orville succeeded him and became president of The Wright Company.

## ⇒ ORVILLE'S LAST DAYS

Orville had a hard time getting over his brother's death. Even though he was president of the Wright Company, he displayed little interest in continuing the business. That summer, he opened up a water flying school in New York. The idea was to fly the airplane out of the water. It was a good idea, but business did not do well. Then an accident occurred when a pilot, Charles Wald, and a woman passenger, Marion G. Peck, crashed into the water. They both survived; however, the water flying school decided to close.

Orville was disappointed. He decided to go back to the shop where he was happiest and invent things. As more people flew, more problems occurred. Unfortunately, in just a short amount of time, several army officers had been killed in different Wright airplanes. Orville received many complaints. He was frustrated because he knew that the crashes could have been avoided. Either the aircraft were not being maintained properly, or the pilots were not flying them correctly. It was becoming more important to make flying as safe as possible. As airplanes continued to develop, other companies built airplanes to compete with the Wright Company.

In October 1915, Orville sold the Wright Company, but stayed on as a consulting engineer. He was paid a yearly salary of $25,000. He also joined the Signal Corps reserve, and worked in their laboratory. But in May 1918, he took his last flight. He flew a 1912 Wright airplane next to a DH-4 to show how far airplanes had come.

Orville was getting older. His father died in 1917 and then Katharine died in 1929. He realized that his family was slowly disappearing and thus kept more to himself.

Orville spent the last thirty years of his life working on inventions in his spare time. Sometimes his inventions were toys for children. One was called Flips and Flops, which his brother Lorin sold nationwide. The toy catapulted a "flying clown" toward bars that the clown would flip around.

## ➲ ACHIEVEMENTS

Many awards were bestowed upon Orville later in life. Orville was a founding member of NACA (National Advisory Committee for Aeronautics). He served on NACA for twenty-eight years. NACA

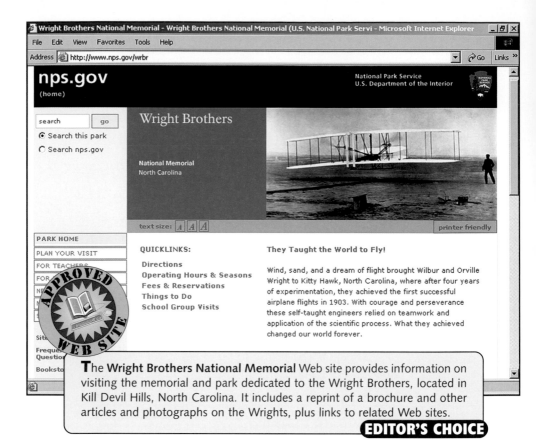

Wright Brothers National Memorial - Wright Brothers National Memorial (U.S. National Park Servi - Microsoft Internet Explorer

File   Edit   View   Favorites   Tools   Help

Address  http://www.nps.gov/wrbr                                                        Go   Links »

**nps.gov**
(home)

National Park Service
U.S. Department of the Interior

search      go
• Search this park
○ Search nps.gov

**Wright Brothers**

National Memorial
North Carolina

text size: A A A                                                        printer friendly

PARK HOME
PLAN YOUR VISIT
FOR TEACHERS
FOR...
N...
M...
Sit...
Freque...
Questio...
Booksto...

QUICKLINKS:

Directions
Operating Hours & Seasons
Fees & Reservations
Things to Do
School Group Visits

**They Taught the World to Fly!**

Wind, sand, and a dream of flight brought Wilbur and Orville
Wright to Kitty Hawk, North Carolina, where after four years
of experimentation, they achieved the first successful
airplane flights in 1903. With courage and perseverance
these self-taught engineers relied on teamwork and
application of the scientific process. What they achieved
changed our world forever.

The **Wright Brothers National Memorial** Web site provides information on
visiting the memorial and park dedicated to the Wright Brothers, located in
Kill Devil Hills, North Carolina. It includes a reprint of a brochure and other
articles and photographs on the Wrights, plus links to related Web sites.

**EDITOR'S CHOICE**

then became NASA (National Aeronautics and
Space Administration) in 1958.

He received the first Daniel Guggenheim
Medal. The Daniel Guggenheim Medal is awarded
for "great achievements in aeronautics."

A monument was erected at Kill Devil Hills to
mark the first flight. Still, the Wrights did not
receive the glory and fame many thought they
deserved. The Smithsonian wanted an original
Wright *Flyer* to hang alongside Langley's *Aerodrome,* but Orville refused. The reason was that the
Smithsonian still considered Langley's airplane to

be the first powered airplane. This problem with the Smithsonian continued for many years. Orville decided to show his airplane in London. This angered many people, but Orville did not care. The dispute with the Smithsonian was finally resolved in 1943. The *Flyer* was returned to the United States five years later and hung in the Smithsonian National Museum.

Orville Wright had a heart attack on January 27, 1948. He died three days later at seventy-six years old. It was a sad day for the people of Dayton. Their hero had died. Schools and shops closed. Flags were hung at half-staff. On the day of his funeral, four fighter jets did a flyby over his grave site.

It was time to bring the Wright *Flyer* home from England. Finally, on December 17, 1948, the 1903 *Flyer* proudly flew in the Smithsonian National Museum. It was exactly forty-five years after the Wrights flew the *Flyer* in Kitty Hawk. It was a great celebration even if the Wright brothers were not a part of it. The Wright brothers finally received the recognition and honor they deserved from the nation's leading scientific institution. The 1903 *Flyer* was home and hanging in the Smithsonian. The Wrights were recognized as the first to conquer the air.

# ACTIVITIES WITH THE WRIGHT BROTHERS IN MIND

The Wright brothers spent many hours studying and testing their kites, gliders, and airplane. Most people do not realize how difficult it was to not only test their ideas, but also to fly a human. Because the Wrights had little money to spend on actually testing their ideas, they spent much of their time calculating and theorizing on paper how something might work. Often, they would build their own machines in order to test them.

## WIND TUNNELS

One of the Wrights' greatest contributions to aviation was the use of the wind tunnel. Since about 1824, wind tunnels had allowed inventors and scientists to study the effects of aerodynamic flow around objects such as scale models and airfoils. Airplanes, cars, and rockets are designed so that the aerodynamic drag is reduced and less fuel is used. Building designs can be tested in wind tunnels to see how much wind a building can withstand before it is damaged.

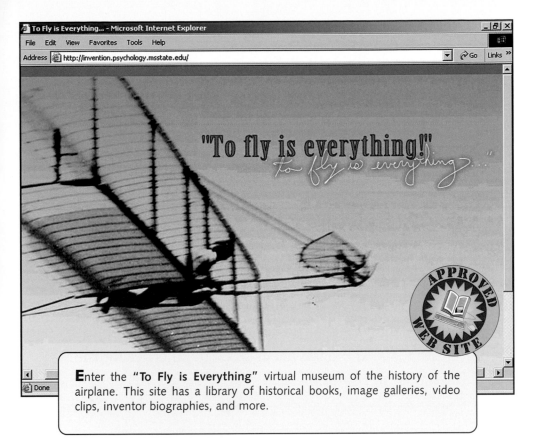

Enter the **"To Fly is Everything"** virtual museum of the history of the airplane. This site has a library of historical books, image galleries, video clips, inventor biographies, and more.

By building a model of an actual airplane, scientists can see how the plane will react to wind while in flight.

### ⊝ MATERIALS NEEDED:

- **3–4 medium-sized cardboard boxes**
- **duct tape**
- **pen, pencil, or marker**
- **ruler**
- **small- to medium-sized scale to measure weight**
- **variable-speed fan**
- **small objects such as pencils, paper clips, cotton ball, die-cast car, balsa wood model airplane.**

109

1. Tape together the boxes with duct tape so that both ends are open.

2. Make one-inch marks on the floor of the boxes to measure the distance an object moves when the wind current (the fan) is applied.

3. Weigh an object and write down the weight. Place the object in the wind tunnel and turn the fan on. How far does the object move at different wind speeds? How do objects at different weights move in the wind tunnel at different wind speeds? Record the distance each object moves and compare.

When using a model airplane, the wind tunnel will allow the airplane to get "lift." Determine what speed the fan needs to be on in order for the model to rise in the air.

## 🧪 AIRFOIL EXPERIMENTS

The Wright brothers understood early on that an airplane lifts into the air and stays there partly because of the air blowing over and under the wings. Make an airfoil wing by trying this experiment.

### ⮕ MATERIALS NEEDED:

- **book**
- **strip of paper (2 inches wide by 10 inches long)**
- **fan**
- **paper clips**

**Wright Brothers: First in Flight**

**O**n this Web site from Discovery Kids you can learn about the Wright Brothers' first flights at Kitty Hawk. View a virtual video of the first four test flights, as well as take a tour of their living quarters.

*Access this Web site from http://www.myreportlinks.com*

1. Place the strip of paper in a book so that the end of the paper is hanging out of the book. Close the book. Blow across the top of the paper. Note how it flutters upward. Have a fan also blow air across it.

2. Take the paper out and hold it against your chin just below your mouth. Blow over the top and see how it rises. Add a paper clip at the end of the paper. Blow again to see how much harder it is to make the paper rise. Add paper clips and try blowing to see how many paper clips can be lifted.

# ACTIVITY #3

## ⚗ THE MAGNUS FLYER

When the Wright brothers received a toy called the Penaud helicopter, they loved to watch it fly. Using a rubber band to give it power, the toy spun into the air and flew. The Magnus Flyer does the same thing. It uses a rubber band to give it power. This is an easy and fun experiment to do. Observe the principles of flight too.

### ⮕ MATERIALS NEEDED:
- **2 Styrofoam cups**
- **tape**
- **rubber band**
- **scissors**

1. Put the two Styrofoam cups bottom to bottom and tape them together. Cut the rubber band so it is one long piece of rubber.

2. Hold the cups sideways and place the rubber band in the middle. Hold it there with your thumb. Pull the rubber band tightly. Wrap it around the center of the cups once. Be sure that the rubber band is now pointing away from you. Pull the rubber band forward and let go of the cups. Watch the Magnus Flyer fly!

3. When the flyer hits the air in front of it, it spins. The air can only go over or under the cups.

The spin on the cups helps the cups grab the air in front of them and carry it over the tops of the cups, similar to a waterwheel. Once the air is behind the cups, the cups dump off the air and shoot it down. Because of the air being pushed down, the cups are pushed up. The air shoots off the cups in one direction, and the cups move in the opposite direction.

# ACTIVITY #4

## ⚗ BUILD AN ANEMOMETER

The Wright brothers were always concerned about the wind. If they did not have enough wind, their glider or airplane could not take off. If there was too much wind, it could crash. They used an anemometer to determine the wind's speed. It is easy to build an anemometer.

## ⮕ MATERIALS NEEDED:

- **5 three–ounce paper cups**
- **paper hole punch**
- **2 straight plastic soda straws**
- **1 straight pin or push pin**
- **1 sharp pencil with an eraser**
- **safety scissors**
- **small stapler**
- **ruler**

1. Take four of the paper cups. Using the paper hole punch, punch one hole in each, about a half inch below the rim.

2. Take the fifth cup. Punch four equally spaced holes about a quarter inch below the rim. Then punch a hole in the center of the bottom of the cup.

3. Take one of the four cups and push a soda straw through the hole. Fold the end of the straw, and staple it to the side of the cup across from the hole. Repeat this procedure for another 1-hole cup and the second straw.

4. Slide one cup and straw assembly through two opposite holes in the cup with four holes. Push another 1-hole cup onto the end of the straw just pushed through the 4-hole cup. Bend the straw and staple it to the 1-hole cup, making certain that the cup faces in the opposite direction from the first cup. Repeat this procedure using the other cup and straw assembly and the remaining 1-hole cup.

5. Align the four cups so that their open ends face in the same direction (clockwise or counterclockwise) around the center cup. Push the straight pin through the two straws where they intersect. Push the eraser end of the pencil through the bottom hole in the center cup. Push the pin into the end of the pencil eraser as far as it will go. The anemometer is ready to use.

▲ *This is an image of a professional anemometer. This device is used to determine the speed of the wind.*

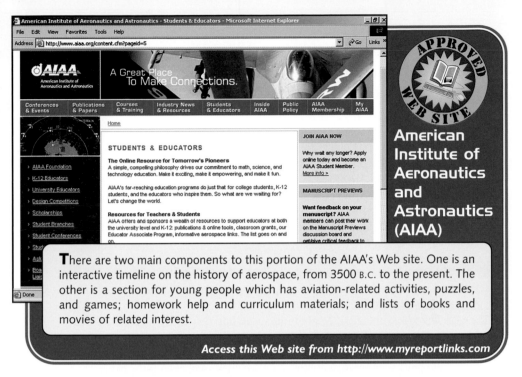

There are two main components to this portion of the AIAA's Web site. One is an interactive timeline on the history of aerospace, from 3500 B.C. to the present. The other is a section for young people which has aviation-related activities, puzzles, and games; homework help and curriculum materials; and lists of books and movies of related interest.

*Access this Web site from http://www.myreportlinks.com*

6. Take the anemometer outside. Watch it spin as the wind strikes it. The anemometer is useful because it rotates with the wind. It does not need to be pointed into the wind to spin.

7. Make a small mark on one of the cups. Record the number of times that cup makes a complete revolution (a complete circle) around the vertical axis (pencil) in a minute. This number will be the revolutions per minute, or RPM. Record your results. Try this at different times in a day or on different days. Record the wind conditions such as no wind, light winds, medium winds, heavy winds, very heavy winds. Is there any pattern that you observe? Does the anemometer spin faster in the morning, afternoon, or evening?

## Report Links

**The Internet sites described below can be accessed at
http://www.myreportlinks.com**

▶**The Wright Brothers & the Invention of the Aerial Age**
\*\*Editor's Choice\*\* Study the lives of the Wright brothers, their accomplishments, and their competitors.

▶**The Wilbur and Orville Wright Papers**
\*\*Editor's Choice\*\* Learn all about the Wright brothers through their writings and pictures.

▶**Wright Brothers National Memorial**
\*\*Editor's Choice\*\* Visit the Wright brothers memorial in Kill Devil Hills, North Carolina.

▶**Wright Brothers' Flying Machine**
\*\*Editor's Choice\*\* Find out about the Wright Brothers and their amazing invention.

▶**U.S. Centennial of Flight Commission**
\*\*Editor's Choice\*\* Celebrate the one hundredth anniversary of the Wright brothers' historic flight.

▶**The Wright Brothers**
\*\*Editor's Choice\*\* Read about the Wright Brothers on this Web site.

▶**Alphonse Penaud**
Alphonse Penaud influenced the Wright brothers when they were at an early age.

▶**American Institute of Aeronautics and Astronautics (AIAA)**
The history of aviation is detailed from 3500 B.C. to the present day.

▶**The Dream of Flight**
Gain an understanding of the Wrights' achievements in the context of world history.

▶**Federal Aviation Administration**
Read about contemporary aviation in the United States.

▶**First Flight**
See how "virtual" models can be used to study flight.

▶**Flights Before the Wrights: Octave Chanute, Chicago**
Learn about Octave Chanute, an important figure in the early history of aviation.

▶**Flights of Inspiration**
Design your own aircraft using the instructional materials on this Web site.

▶**George Cayley**
This online resume profiles a nineteenth-century aviator and his glider.

▶**George Spratt**
Aviation pioneer George Spratt worked with the Wrights.

MyReportLinks.com Books

# Report Links

## The Internet sites described below can be accessed at http://www.myreportlinks.com

▶**How Airplanes Work**
Discover how airplanes work.

▶**John Smeaton**
Learn about the engineer responsible for "Smeaton's Coefficient."

▶**Leonardo Da Vinci**
Read about Leonardo Da Vinci and his plans for flying machines.

▶**National Air and Space Museum**
View online exhibits about Washington, D.C.'s Air and Space Museum.

▶**National Aviation Hall of Fame**
Browse bios of all the important figures from the history of aviation.

▶**The Octave Chanute Pages**
First-hand accounts of experiments done by this pioneering aviator.

▶**OhioLINK Digital Media Center: Wright Brothers Collection**
View this collection of Wright Brothers images on this site.

▶**Otto Lilienthal**
Learn more about Otto Lilienthal, inventor of the glider.

▶**Samuel Pierpont Langley**
The Langley *Aerodrome* was an early aircraft made by this competitor of the Wright brothers.

▶***TIME* 100: The Wright Brothers**
Read a profile of the Wright Brothers on this Web site from *Time* magazine.

▶**"To Fly is Everything!"**
Study aviation through inventor profiles, simulations, and more.

▶**Wright Brothers Centennial Exhibit**
Browse this Wright Brothers collection from East Carolina University.

▶**Wright Brothers: First in Flight**
View this interactive site about the first flight at Kitty Hawk.

▶**The Wright Brothers: Pioneers in Aviation**
The Smithsonian Institute summarizes the career of the Wright Brothers at this Web site.

▶**The Wright Experience**
Read about the efforts of a group that replicates the Wrights' work a century later.

**aerodynamics**—The study of air flow and how it affects an object, like an airplane.

**ailerons**—Moveable surfaces, usually near the tip of the wing. They control the roll and bank of an airplane.

**airfoils**—The surface of a propeller blade or wing whose shape controls stability, thrust, lift, and propulsion.

**anemometer**—A device that calculates the speed of the wind and also measures the force of the wind.

**drag**—The aerodynamic force against an aircraft that reduces its forward motion.

**elevator**—The horizontal surface, usually at the rear of an airplane (the *Flyer's* was in the front), that controls pitch.

**equilibrium**—When an aircraft is balanced because of two equal opposing forces.

**fatality**—The death of a person after he or she has suffered a tragedy, such as a violent accident.

**glider**—A motorless aircraft that uses wind currents to fly.

**lift**—Upward motion of an object when it is pushed by air.

**Outer Banks**—A section of North Carolina consisting of a series of islands and sandy beaches along the state's Atlantic coast.

**pitch**—The motion of the nose of the plane as it goes up or down.

**roll**—The motion of an aircraft's wing tipping up or down.

**shinny**—A game like hockey which is usually played on ice. Players use a curved stick instead of a standard hockey stick and a ball or block of wood instead of a hockey puck. The stick itself is also called a shinny.

**stabilizer**—An airfoil that controls stability.

**telegram**—A typed and sent over an electronic wire and then received and typed out at the other end. With modern telephones and electric communications such as e-mail and text messaging, telegrams are rarely sent.

**torque**—A twisting force.

**tuberculosis**—An infectious disease that affects the lungs.

**wind tunnel**—Device used to measure the effect of wind on certain objects such as wings, airfoils, buildings, and cars.

**wing warp**—The ability to move the wings in order to stay aloft to have lift.

**yaw**—To have motion about a vertical axis.

## Chapter 1. Take to the Skies

1. First Flight, "Part II—Achieving the Dream," *The Franklin Institute,* n.d., <http://www.fi.edu/flights /first/intro.html> (July 27, 2006).

2. Ibid.

3. Marvin W. Kranz, "Telegram, Orville Wright to Bishop Milton Wright announcing the first successful powered flight, 17 December [1903]," *Library of Congress—American Memory,* n.d., <http:// memory.loc.gov/cgi-bin/query/r?ammem/mcc: @field(DOCID+@lit(mcc/061))> (July 27, 2006).

## Chapter 2. Childhood Dreams

1. The Wright Brothers—The Invention of the Aerial Age, "Who were Wilbur and Orville?" *Smithsonian National Air and Space Museum,* n.d., <http://www.nasm.si.edu/wrightbrothers/who/1859 /index.cfm> (December 12, 2006).

2. First Flight, "Part I—Inventing the Future," *Franklin Institute,* n.d., <http://sln.fi.edu/flights /first/before.html> (December 12, 2006).

3. Fred C. Kelly, *The Wright Brothers: A Biography* (New York: Dover Publications, 1989), p. 28.

4. James Tobin, *To Conquer the Air: The Wright Brothers and the Great Race for Flight* (New York: Simon and Schuster Adult Publishing Group, 2003), p. 41.

5. Gary Bradshaw, "Wilbur and Orville Wright," *The Wright House,* n.d., <http://www.wright-house .com/wright-brothers/> (December 12, 2006).

6. The Dream of Flight, "Image," *American Library of Congress,* n.d., <http://www.loc.gov/exhibits /treasures/images/wbf0010p1s.jpg> (July 7, 2006).

7. Personal interview with former Naval Flight Officer, Jeff Reed, August 26, 2006.

## Chapter 3. Gliding into Flight

1. Jean Paul Richter, *The Notebooks of Leonardo Da Vinci—Volume II* (New York: Dover Publications Inc., 1970), p. 278.

2. Carroll Gray, "Sir George Cayley: 1773–1857," *FlyingMachines.org,* n.d., <http://www.flyingmachines .org/cayl.html> (December 12, 2006).

3. Ibid.

4. First Flight, "Part I—Inventing the Future," *Franklin Institute,* n.d., <http://sln.fi.edu/flights /first/before.html> (December 13, 2006).

5. James Tobin, *To Conquer the Air: The Wright Brothers and the Great Race for Flight* (New York: Simon and Schuster Adult Publishing Group, 2003), p. 102.

6. Ibid., p. 106.

7. Ibid., p. 112.

8. Ibid., p. 113.

## Chapter 4. Gliding to Success

1. Conversation with former Naval Flight Officer, Jeff Reed, July 17, 2006.

2. First Flight, "Part I—Inventing the Future," *Franklin Institute,* n.d., <http://sln.fi.edu/flights /first/before.html> (December 13, 2006).

3. First Flight, "The Airfoils," *Franklin Institute,* n.d., <http://sln.fi.edu/flights/first/foil1.html> (December 13, 2006).

4. Tom D. Crouch, *Bishop's Boys: A Life of Wilbur and Orville Wright* (New York: Norton, W.W. and Company, 1989), p. 228.

5. Fred C. Culick and Spencer Dunmore, *On Great White Wings: The Wright Brothers and the Race for Flight* (New York: Hyperion, 2001), p. 51.

6. Ibid.

7. First Flight, "Part I—Inventing the Future," *Franklin Institute,* n.d., <http://sln.fi.edu/flights /first/before.html> (December 13, 2006).

## Chapter 5. Birth of the Airplane

1. Fred C. Culick and Spencer Dunmore, *On Great White Wings: The Wright Brothers and the Race for Flight* (New York: Hyperion, 2001), p. 56.

2. Ibid., p. 59.

3. Fred C. Kelly, *The Wright Brothers: A Biography* (New York: Dover Publications, 1989), p. 89.

4. Culick and Dunmore, p. 71.

5. James Tobin, *To Conquer the Air: The Wright Brothers and the Great Race for Flight* (New York: Simon and Schuster Adult Publishing Group, 2003), p. 182.

## Chapter 6. Age of Flight

1. Fred C. Culick and Spencer Dunmore, *On Great White Wings: The Wright Brothers and the Race for Flight* (New York: Hyperion, 2001), p. 82.

2. Ibid., p. 89.

3. Fred C. Kelly, *The Wright Brothers: A Biography* (New York: Dover Publications, 1989), p. 239.

4. Fred C. Kelly, ed., *Miracle at Kitty Hawk: The Letters of Wilbur and Orville Wright* (Cambridge, Mass.: Da Capo Press, 1996), p. 296.

5. Culick and Dunmore, p. 122.

6. Ibid., p. 155.

## Activities With the Wright Brothers

Activity 1—Wind Tunnels, NASA, (http://observe.arc.nasa.gov/nasa/education/teach_guide/tunnel.html#act).

Activity 2—Airfoils, Aeronautics Learning Laboratory for Science, Technology, and Research, (http://www.allstar.fiu.edu/aero/Experiment1.htm).

Activity 3—The Magnus Flyer, (http://sln.fi.edu/Wright/magnus.html).

Activity 4—Wright Again, Build an Anemometer, (http://wings.avkids.com/Book/Wright/lesson2_19011.html).

Busby, Peter. *First to Fly: How Wilbur and Orville Wright Invented the Airplane.* New York: Crown, 2002.

Carson, Mary Kay. *The Wright Brothers for Kids: How They Invented the Airplane—21 Activities Exploring the Science and History of Flight.* Chicago, Ill.: Chicago Review Press, 2003.

Collins, Mary. *Airborne: A Photobiography of Wilbur and Orville Wright.* Washington D.C.: National Geographic, 2003.

Ford, Carin T. *The Wright Brothers: Heroes of Flight.* Berkeley Heights, N.J.: Enslow Publishers, 2005.

Hansen, Ole Steen. *The Wright Brothers and Other Pioneers of Flight.* New York: Crabtree Pub., 2003.

Hossell, Karen Price. *Kitty Hawk: The Flight of the Wright Brothers.* Chicago, Ill.: Heinemann Library, 2003.

McPherson, Stephanie Sammartino and Joseph Sammartino Gardner. *Wilbur and Orville Wright: Taking Flight.* Minneapolis: Carolrhoda Books, 2004.

O'Brien, Patrick. *Fantastic Flights: One Hundred Years of Flying on the Edge.* New York: Walker & Company, 2003.

Old, Wendie C. *The Wright Brothers: Inventors of the Airplane.* Berkeley Heights, N.J.: Enslow Publishers, 2000.

Rinard, Judith E. *The Story of Flight: The Smithsonian National Air and Space Museum.* Willowdale, Ont.: Firefly Books, 2002.